FAITHFULLY
Yours

In Loving Memory of My Darling Wife Shashi

RAVI DASS

Paperback: 978-1-965632-31-4
eBook: 978-1-965632-32-1
Library of Congress Control Number: 2024920715

Ordering Information:

Prime Seven Media
518 Landmann St.
Tomah City, WI 54660

Printed in the United States of America

As God is my witness, I love you more than I can say I want to be your companion for eternity and a day My life with you has been full of joy and happiness Without you I am in the dark, empty wilderness The emptiness that has been created by your leaving Will be impossible to fill with any real meaning I pray to God that I will be worthy of a place in heaven Where I know you will be So that I can spend all of eternity and a day With you my darling Shashi.

Dedication

In loving memory of my dear beloved wife, Shashi, who passed away on 22 May 2011, after a prolonged illness. I loved her more than I can ever express and more than life itself. She always wanted me to finish this book, which I had started writing in 2005. This book has been completed and dedicated to you, my darling, under circumstances that are painful. I wish I had finished it while you were still alive and had the opportunity to read it. It would have made you so happy and proud. I will always love you and cherish your loving memory. Thank you for making my life so wonderful. I love you, darling, and always will. May your soul rest in peace.

PREFACE

I had always wanted to write a book of a serious and meaningful nature. Thoughts of God, His teachings and what He wanted from us had always been a part of my contemplation and I wanted to write about the reflections of my conscience and soul.

One day I felt the urge to put my thoughts down on paper. The feeling was so overwhelming that I started to write, and kept on writing for about an hour, almost nonstop. Thoughts – from where they came, I did not know – started flowing of their own free will and gave me the basis of what I wanted to write.

At that first time of writing, I wanted an opinion from someone I respected, about whether my subject had any merit in order for me to continue or would it be just a waste of my time. I needed this assurance as this was the first time I had endeavored to put pen to paper in such a manner, to write a book.

I wrote a short introduction about the contents and general direction I wanted my book to take and then gave the pages to Sally Kirby, a friend and colleague, to let me know what she thought about the subject I had chosen and my chances of writing a readable and interesting book. Sally was very supportive and encouraged me to continue writing.

This book is a work of fiction, written in story form. It represents my ideas of what God wants from us and how the world can be made a better place for all to live in. Whether you agree with my ideas and thoughts expressed in this book is entirely up to you. I will respect your views as I hope you will mine.

Ravi Dass

ACKNOWLEDGEMENT

I am thankful to Sally Kirby, a colleague and a good friend, for her support. She has been a sounding board for my thoughts on the subject of the book and has encouraged me at every stage. Sally was the first person from whom I sought an opinion regarding the subject matter and desire to write the book.

When I told my family about what I was intending to write, they were very supportive and thrilled. At times when I was rather lethargic, they pushed me to continue and finish the book.

Without the encouragement of Sally and my family, I would not have persevered and finished the book. In-fact, it has made me think about writing other materials, perhaps short stories, related to things that I feel strongly about.

I had stopped writing, midway, for a long time. Tragically, it took the passing away of my dear wife, Shashi, to compel me to finish the book in her loving memory.

CONTENTS

BOOK 1

CHAPTER 1

Introduction

L et me state from the outset that the thoughts and statements in this book are my own. They are not based on any fact, but my personal thinking on the matters I have decided to write about. Some people may not agree with my views, but all I ask of them is to think about my underlying thoughts; to reflect on them, because I believe they have a valid point to make.

The story that unfolds later in this book, again, is my impression of the meaning of God to mankind and what He would want from us, if we accept that He really exists. I believe that there can only be one God and therefore all religions incorporate His teachings. To deny any one belief is to deny God.

It is a difficult topic to write on, as any definite conclusion is next to impossible. The belief in God is faith, and faith is individual and unique to each person. I am not trying to belittle anybody's faith or belief in God but trying to put my own perspective regarding His existence and meaning. I am certain of one thing: all that is preached, stated or done in the name of God, He would not approve of. We humans tend to do things in His name to justify our actions, even if they are wrong. These are my feelings for which I make no apologies.

Who or what is 'God'? When we are infants, we are told that God, who is goodness personified, lives somewhere up in the sky in a place called heaven. The opposite of God is known as Satan, who is evil, residing in a place called hell which is somewhere down below, though we are not told where, as nobody is quite sure. I have used the Christian belief in this statement although these basic thoughts and teachings are religiously universal.

When we get older and begin to ask searching questions about what we had been told in our youth, we are then told that God is in spirit form, not human. God created the world and is in fact our 'Father in Heaven'. God is the good and decent side of our existence, whereas Satan is the bad and evil side of ourselves. If we submit to the bad and evil side of ourselves, we will go to hell where we will suffer, in damnation, throughout our 'life after death'; whereas if we live according to the laws and the will of God we will go to heaven where we will live with God in eternal bliss.

All major religions of the world have Holy Scriptures, which have been handed down throughout the ages, telling us about God, what He expects from us and how He wants us to live our lives. Every religion seems to think that their belief in God and His existence is the only real and correct concept. This is where confusion, intolerance and quarrels start.

Why cannot the various 'religions' in this world understand that the concept of God can only mean one God? If we accept the view that God exists, then the next step is to assume that God has manifested Himself to us humans in various forms in relation to the various regions of the world and their customs and ability to understand Him. There can only be one God, and basically all religions have similar teachings in their Scriptures. Why then the need for people of one religion to force their version to people of other religions? This causes bad feelings, quarrels and misunderstandings. In-fact many wars in our history have been fought in the name of religion. This surely is not what God intended. Certainly, war against evil, but not against different religious beliefs! All religious beliefs lead to the one and only God.

Surely the most obvious, sensible and logical thing would be to accept that, as there can only be one God, all religions are in tune with Him, therefore there is no need to try and convert people of other religions to one's way of thinking. All one needs to do is to tell all people that they should follow the law of God as set out in the religion they have been brought up in. Everyone should convey the message of God, which is the same in all religions on basic and fundamental matters.

Perhaps the above suggestion is too easy or too complex for the clergy of the various religions. Their authority will decrease if they did not feel it necessary to decry other religious beliefs. I feel that many of the people who preach, try to sustain their authority by making religion too complex, in order to maintain their standing in the public eye.

I also think that interpretation of the Scriptures through the ages has changed the essence of the original message of God. Religion has become a very large and lucrative industry and does not seem to have anything to do with God and certainly nothing to do with faith in God. It is too much about 'me and my religion' from the clergy or so-called preachers of the various religions. There does not seem to be any togetherness.

Having said all the above, the question arises; does God exist? Who has seen God? All the Scriptures could have been written by authors who had written great works. There have been a number of such people throughout the history of mankind. Certainly, the Scriptures have been written by great minds, but I believe, under the guidance of God with His enlightened disclosures, channelled through those great minds.

There have been certain facts and events that give food for thought. How did the many religious Scriptures, having almost identical views and laws for life get written by different people, at a time when communication as we know it, was not available? How did similar thoughts get into the minds of the various people who wrote the Scriptures? This simple direction of thought gives rise to the feeling that perhaps something similar happened in various parts of the world that gave rise to similar thought. This gives credence to the assumption that God manifested Himself in various ways in various different parts of the world and this had been written, in the Scriptures of various religions, by the great minds of that time. God is omnipresent and so it is not difficult to imagine His presence throughout the world with all manner of people with different cultures, giving understanding to people within that culture of the one and only God.

At the end of the day, belief in God is pure faith. There is no concrete evidence that God exists. Things have happened in this world, which people have taken as God's doing, but in a world that is large and complex, these can also be taken as pure coincidence, luck or something which can not be explained at that moment in time. But the miracle of life and human intelligence can only really be explained by the belief in the existence of God.

Perhaps mankind needs to believe in God for its sanity and comfort, like a child needs the reassurance and comfort of a parent to allay its fears and forebodings, to feel that someone is there to give a helping hand when things get difficult. Without this reassurance perhaps mankind would feel that no one is there to look after them in times of difficulties. Perhaps we need the strength of a father figure to exist, from whom we can ask for forgiveness when we do something wrong and to whom we can turn for help in times of need. Belief in God gives great strength and comfort and enables us to face the problems of daily life.

If life has problems, it is made easier to bear if one believes in God. The belief that God will hear our prayers and help us, is necessary for sanity. Everyone has their problems, some more acute than others. The faith that things will improve through God's help allows us to move ahead in life. Even if no such help comes our way and things do not change for the better, the faith that they will in the future allows us to carry on. Unfortunately, for many people, this hope stays alive without any change until they die. Many live in misery all their lives in the belief God will have mercy, but this remains a hope and never materializes. This is where the 'father figure' concept of God comes in. Hope is a very important part of life, without which living would be very difficult and possibly impossible. Without hope there is no life.

If one could have an audience with God, there would be so many questions to ask for which there are no answers at present. The answers would enable us to understand more clearly, why certain things happen and be guided as to how we should live our lives. Certainly, our faith in God would be strengthened.

This leads me to the book I am writing. It is in story form. God is not depicted to be from any religion. The thoughts and conclusions are entirely my own. They have not been arrived at frivolously; they represent deep-rooted thoughts and I have arrived at such conclusions with a great deal of logic and soul-searching.

I am a family man, with a wife and two grown-up children, all of whom I love dearly. As with most families we also have our problems and as with most people, we consider our problems to be the most serious.

In my case, the problems encompass my whole family. These problems have been present for a considerable number of years. Nothing seems to improve fundamentally. I find it difficult to know what to do or whom to turn to. Perhaps some of the problems are of my own doing, but certain things had happened, for which I did not make any allowances. This has resulted in my present dilemma. In these circumstances my faith in that God exists keeps me optimistic that things will turn out for the better in time. Without His help, directly or indirectly, I see little solution to these problems. Things have gone along somehow, but a stage is arriving where something has to happen otherwise things will come to a head. Certain miraculous events have happened in my past, which have allowed me breathing space. I can only attribute these helpful events as a result of the intervention by God. I am sure that God will be there for me when I really need Him. This is the faith that keeps me going. I have only mentioned this to pave the way for the story about to unfold. I will not go into details of my problems, as this is not the subject of this book. The various problems that I have been facing and am still facing have made me think, in great depth, about God and what He means to me and to the rest of mankind, and what faith can do in creating the hope that is necessary for living our lives. It is with this background that I have written this story.

CHAPTER 2

The Awakening

When I go to bed, at the early stages my sleep tends to be disturbed due to my worries, and the many thoughts I invariably have. However, this is also the time when my thoughts seem to be at their clearest. Although thoughts about God always occur, recently they have been more frequent and more pronounced, with a great deal more clarity. Perhaps this is because I feel that the only solution to my problems that I can see is with the help of God. I have felt that I needed to renew and strengthen my faith in God in order to hold on to the hope that there will be a positive change in my circumstances.

Recently while in bed, I imagined that God came into my dreams, and I started asking Him many questions to which I desperately needed answers. God told me that these questions were the same that all people wanted the answers to. He said that it had been a long time since He had direct contact with the people of earth, and it was time He manifested Himself again to the people, so that their faith in Him could be strengthened. He said that with all that was happening in our world, people were losing faith in Him. They were preoccupied with materialistic things, achieving targets, reaching their goals and living a fast lifestyle. They did not have time for

Him and yet expected that He would make all things right for them. When this did not happen, and which they should not have expected in the first place, they only gave Him lip service and did not really follow all of His laws sincerely, but only the ones that did not require sacrifices by them. He also felt that we were too engrossed with the word 'religion', twisting religious teachings to conform to our ideas, concepts and desires thereby forgetting the meaning of God and concentrating on our own interests and religious differences, which actually had no meaning.

All these thoughts were running through my mind for a number of days, and my sleeping thoughts were totally on God. An idea began to take shape in my mind regarding what my sub-conscious was trying to convey to me. I started to feel that I had to put my thoughts and concepts down on paper and try to get some clear picture about God and His place in our lives. This feeling started to blossom into ideas as to how I should convey this in a book. Finally, I decided that it would be in a story format, which would be more readable and would allow me to use my conscience as a guide for God to give answers to the questions that were generally asked by humans. The questions to God and his answers are not definitive, but reflect my ability, based on my conscience, to find an answer that God would consider reasonable, according to His laws and teachings.

It required a great deal of thought and soul-searching to find the right way for me to get my thoughts on paper, without unnecessarily incensing people. Finally, I found the way that would make it possible to write the book in a manner suited to my personality, thoughts and possible talents.

My thoughts about God are told in a story format with myself as the character liaising with God. All other names used are fictitious.

CHAPTER 3

Contact with God

One night, I spoke to God. While trying to get to sleep, I heard a voice, not audible but registering within my mind.

The voice seemed to say, "Ravi, I want you to do something for me. I want you to arrange for an interview with me that can be heard by all the people on earth."

The voice startled me as it seemed so real, but I felt that my mind was playing tricks.

Again, "You do not seem to believe your own mind. I am whom you call 'God'. What I am saying is real, not an illusion. Recently you have been thinking a great deal about me and my meaning to you and mankind. Due to the sincerity of your thoughts, I have chosen you for the task at hand. Think about what you have heard and do whatever is necessary to get things done according to what I want carried out by you."

Hearing the same voice again, I was truly convinced of the reality of what my mind was registering.

My mind automatically responded, "God, in order for me to carry out your bidding I will need to know what the purpose of such an interview will be."

God said, "I want the world to know that I AM. The world does not seem to be convinced of my existence and how I want them to conduct themselves. They seem to go about unsure as to why they should believe in me. There are so many questions I am sure they would like to ask, that will help them in their realisation of my existence and how they should live their lives. Once you have set the ball rolling, as you earth people would express it, we will work out a detailed agenda. In the meantime, go and talk to television and radio networks to get them interested in broadcasting the interview." A thought occurred to me. "If I go and talk about what you have stated, people will not take me seriously. They will laugh at me and consider me mad. I need some miracle performed on these network bosses that will convince them that what I am saying is to be taken seriously. Even then, they could construe any miracle as a trick. I am sure however that with your help and guidance this too will present no difficulty."

God said, "I had thought of this and the way to convince people can be effective in the following manner: tell the network people you talk to, that they should have ten different people speaking ten different languages to listen to your conversation with them. These people should speak and understand only their own language and no other. You will speak to all of them at the same time in Latin, which is a classical language known to hardly anybody except some scholars. But they will all understand what you are saying, despite the fact that they cannot speak or understand Latin. Tell them that the final broadcast will be in the same format, no interpretation will be necessary, as all people listening to the broadcast will understand. This fact should be made known at the beginning of the broadcast so that all people listening are aware of the miracle being performed.

Such miracles should not be necessary for people to believe in me, but because the faith of mankind appears to be fickle, this is needed."

"God, I do no speak or understand Latin, so how can I convey myself in this language?"

"You do not have to worry yourself about this. When the time comes you will be able to convey your message in Latin."

I realised that this simple solution to the query I had raised would indeed convince people of the reality of what I was saying. I also realised that this would also totally convince me of the reality of my conversation with God. If I were to pull this off, it would mean that God had really spoken to me.

CHAPTER 4

The Arrangement

I set about my task with vigour. I tried to find out addresses and phone numbers of large TV networks in the USA and the UK. I knew that I had to talk directly with people high up in the various networks I wanted to contact. If I could convince one network, then other networks would present no problem. Since I was living in the UK, I decided to contact the Chairman of the WCN (World Communications Network). It would be an uphill task to even get to speak to the Chairman, let alone convince him of what I intended to do. However, with God helping me, I felt that I would succeed.

I dialed the phone number of WCN headquarters at Broadcasting House in London. A voice said, "Hallo, this is the WCN. My name is Diane Hopkins. How can I help you?" I said, "I would like to talk to the Chairman. Can you put me through to his secretary?"

"Is the Chairman expecting your call?"

"No, the Chairman is not expecting my call, but I would, however, like to speak with him, if that is at all possible. It is rather urgent, and I am sure he would wish to speak to me." "I will find out if he will talk to you. Please tell me the nature of your query and your name." "My name is Ravi Dass. What I have to say is private and urgent."

"Please hold, while I contact his secretary."

After a few minutes I was put through to the Chairman's secretary.

"This is Sally Burgess, Mr. Dass, how can I help you?"

"I wish to talk to the Chairman, please."

"Could you tell me the nature of your business, Mr. Dass?"

"What I have to talk about is rather private and I should really only disclose this to him."

"Do not worry; I am privy to all conversation by the Chairman. I will need to know the nature of your business to be able to put you through to him."

"I want to arrange a TV interview with God on the WCN. Please don't hang up. I am not a crank. I am perfectly serious. If I can talk to the Chairman, I will prove to him the truth about what I have just stated. I know what I have said sounds unbelievable, but please allow the Chairman to judge the validity of what I have stated. If he wishes, I can prove it right now on the telephone."

I think God must have influenced the secretary and the Chairman to listen to me because the next thing I heard was the voice of a man, whom I presumed to be the Chairman.

"Hallo Mr. Dass, it is difficult for me to accept what you say. But due to its sheer absurdity I'm curious to see how you are going to prove the validity of your claim, and because of some unknown compulsion, I will give you two minutes to convince me of the truth of what you have stated to my secretary."

I chose my words carefully.

"God has asked me to arrange an interview with Him to be broadcast to all people in this world. In order to prove that what I'm saying is the truth, God will perform a miracle. Please arrange for ten people speaking ten different languages. These people should only speak and understand their own language and no other. I will speak in Latin, although I do not understand or speak a word of it. This in itself will be a miracle. As Latin is an almost extinct language, it is unlikely that any of the ten people understand it. But each and every one of them will. This will be the miracle to prove that God really exists and wants this interview to take place. I will leave my contact details with your secretary so that when you have arranged for the persons to be present, you can contact me, and I can speak to them. This is not some sort of a joke or in any way a prank. It will be a world-changing event so please take it seriously. I implore you to give me this one chance to prove what I have said."

I held my breath, although I need not have done. God was obviously helping me to set this up.

"Alright, Mr. Dass, I will do as you have asked in order for you to prove your claim. I will arrange for ten people having no knowledge of Latin or any language other than their own. I will need a few days to find the appropriate people and set up the necessary communication system. When I have arranged this, I will contact you and let you know the time and date this will take place. I will leave you now as a great deal has to be arranged. Goodbye for now."

I was relieved that the process had started, and the interview would, in time, be a reality. Speaking in Latin to illustrate the reality of the instructions given by God was to give extra credence to the demonstration. The actual interview with God would be carried out in English, as I would be speaking from England. Now that I was sure of the interview, many thoughts started going through my mind. How would the clergy of various religions take it? First of all, they would not believe it. They would denounce it as blasphemy and would try to cause an outcry and condemnation; and secondly, even if they did believe it to be true, they would not accept that a mere nobody, having no credentials of any religious order, was chosen for this by God. It was going to be a difficult period prior to the interview. I was sure that a great many angry phone calls and letters would be received by the WCN in this regard demanding to know why it was involving itself in this charade. But I soon realised that the ease with which all that had happened up to this stage was truly amazing. Hence, I was not too worried about the outcry, knowing that when the time came, I would be able to find the right words to deal with whatever was thrown at me and if necessary, God would help me by performing another miracle. Some would be convinced while others, who felt threatened, would need more convincing or would not want to be convinced because they did not really believe in God, but were using His name for their own purposes and the power it gave them. This small number of people, in my view, were not worth convincing. I was sure things would resolve themselves though God's help. Another important thing to arrange for was to get a list of questions that people wanted to ask God, so that these could be incorporated in the interview.

I had decided that I would ask the various networks worldwide to request people who wanted answers from God, to send in their questions. These could then be sorted, and the relevant ones could be given to me and a few others to weed out the frivolous ones, leaving a set of questions that basically covered all that most people wanted the answers to.

That night, after having talked to the Chairman of the WCN, I relayed to God what I had been doing and the progress that had been made. Not because God would not already know, but so that I could clear my thoughts regarding on what had been achieved and what more had to be done before the interview took place. A great deal of work still had to be carried out before the broadcast of the interview.

"God, I have been able to convince the Chairman of the WCN, no doubt through your help, to take the suggestion for an interview seriously. He is making the necessary arrangements for my talk to ten people. The miracle can then be performed, so that he is fully convinced. There have been a few things that have been troubling me with regard to the interview, though. The clergy of the various religious orders are going to be livid and up in arms when they get to hear of this. Some answers, that they are willing to accept, will have to be given to them otherwise it can create problems. All genuine clergy will, I am sure, be convinced because of their true belief in You, whereas others who use religion for their own ends will not accept that You have chosen me to carry out Your bidding. These will be small in numbers with whom we will have to put up with as their views have no real value to true religious believers. I will also ask the various networks, through the WCN, to relay to the world that such an interview with You will be taking place and that people should send in the questions that they want to ask."

God said, "I realise that certain genuine clergymen and others, not so genuine followers of the various religious orders will be angry with what is being proposed, as their thinking about who I am and their role in spreading my word is somewhat different from what I would want. After listening to the broadcast, a number of them, who really want to spread my word will see the truth in what is happening, whereas others who are not genuine will not want to be convinced as their purpose in using religion for their personal gain will be endangered. But regardless of such people, I want the message to go out to all mankind. It is for them to understand the message and relate to it in the way they live. With regard to the questions people want to ask, you will need to weed out the frivolous ones from the genuine ones."

"There is going to be an angry outcry from the various religious bodies at me. How do I handle this and not allow them to hamper what is being planned?"

"You know what I want and will be able to answer anyone who questions what is being done. I have complete trust in your capacity and diplomacy to handle any such situation that may arise. I will be with you every step of the way."

"I thank You, God, in your faith in me. I will do my utmost in implementing Your wishes. I am sure that I will find the right words when I have to answer issues raised by the clergy on my genuine credentials to do your bidding. "

After this I slept peacefully without any worries or further mental disturbance.

When I woke up the next morning, I realised that it may take a few days before the Chairman of WCN contacted me, so I utilised my time in thinking about exactly what needed to be done and how it should be set up. I also thought about the kind of questions that people would wish to ask God. I started by writing down the questions that I wanted to ask. I was sure that my questions would not be far different from the questions being asked by other people. At least it was a starting point and would keep me busy until I heard from the Chairman.

The next few days were spent in reading about the various different religious teachings and what their Scriptures stated. This was necessary to make sure that what I was saying would not offend anyone in any major way. Also, I would be a little more equipped to answer the questions that would come once my intentions were made public. Clearly the time span was not enough to know everything about every religion, but it would give me some ideas and knowledge, which I am sure would be useful in the days to come.

I started listing the things that had to be done and the sequence of doing them. It was not just a matter of convincing the various people concerned of what required to be done, but also showing them how it should be done. A plan had to be drawn up to make the whole thing possible. It was not going to be easy in relaying the message of God to all and sundry on earth. It required elaborate and effective preparation.

Of course, at the end of the day, help from God would always be there otherwise it would not be possible to achieve what was required. The logistics were too great.

I was in employment at the time, and I had to do all the planning in my spare time, usually evenings and weekends. I did, however, contact the various people by telephone during the daytime. I had decided that if more time was needed during working hours, I would take part of my annual leave. More time and effort would be needed once the WCN or any other large network took the idea of an interview with God seriously. I was sure that this would happen and fairly soon, so that the logistics and agenda of this program could be worked out.

With the above in mind, I started jotting down any points that came to mind that could help in the preparations. I would collate all the questions, my own and others received from the various people around the world into a list. I would then relay this list to God, to ask Him whether He approved of them. A few days later I got a call from the WCN. "This is Sally Burgess from the WCN. Am I speaking to Mr. Dass?"

"Yes, this is Mr. Dass speaking,"

"The Chairman wants to talk to you, Mr. Dass. Please hold while I connect you to him."

The Chairman came on the line. "Mr. Dass, I have made the arrangements as you specified. I have ten people here who only speak and understand their own language. Also, I have a number of interpreters, who will ask them what they heard after you have spoken. If what you have stated is true, then all of them will have the same answer. There is also a tape recorder so that your exact words are recorded and can be played back to the people here in case they forget anything you say. Come to the WCN headquarters tomorrow at 2.30 in the afternoon and you will be directed to a room set up with a microphone to give your speech to the ten people, who will be listening to you over a loudspeaker in another room. The time for your speech is 3 in the afternoon. The ball is now in your court."

Sally then came on the line and gave me instructions to get to the studio. The moment had come. This was the time when even I would have definite proof of my contact with God and of His existence. It was really not necessary as I was fully convinced of the reality of my talks with God and His wishes for me to carry out His bidding. It was, however, very reassuring to have this additional proof.

I arrived at the WCN headquarters at 2.30 in the afternoon the next day. On reaching the reception desk, I was recognised and taken into a room from where I was to talk. I looked at the arrangements made and the set of microphones into which I had to speak. While waiting for 3pm to arrive I looked into the notes I had made to make sure that I had covered all that I wanted to say. My notes were in

English, but once I started speaking, I would be heard in Latin. Finally, the time to start speaking to convey my message had arrived. Mi homo iste, quid tibi aegre potest credi, sed quid dicat finem, vos credimus. "My fellow human beings, what I have to tell you may be difficult to believe, but by the end of what I have to say, you will also believe."

I paused for a moment and then continued. Instructus sum ab illo Deo disponere colloquium broadcast omnicoach hominicoach. Ut homines ad Deum vere cognoscimus quod dicturus est eis, non dolo, quamvis omnes intelligunt quod ait, ut lingua loqui, quod nunquam audivi numerum eorum ante. Donavit mihi Deus in hoc illustretur per potestatem super te. Vos mos quoque quamvis intelligam quod dico ut nemo vos dicere nec intelligere lingua loquor. Lingua exstincta est, nisi ubi paucis cognoscenda hominum, et loqui in omni fiducia. Nescio Latine uno verbo, nedum dicere, non me audies et Latine sciunt et credunt miracula faciendo Deum. "I have been instructed by God to arrange an interview with Him to be broadcast to all of mankind. In order for mankind to know that it is not just a trick, they will all understand what He says despite the fact that He may be speaking a language that a number of them may never have heard before. God has given me this same power to illustrate the effect on you. You will also understand what I am saying despite the fact that none of you speak or understand the language I am speaking. I do not know a single word of Latin, let alone speak it, yet you will hear me speak in Latin and know the miracle God is performing and believe."

After having delivered this speech, I went to the receptionist to put me through to the Chairman on the phone.

"Hallo, this is Sally Burgess. May I know who is calling?" "This is Ravi Dass; please could you put me through to the Chairman."

"Yes, of course, Mr. Dass. Please hold on a second."

The Chairman came on and said, "Hallo Mr. Dass. How did your transmission go?"

I paused, then said, "Mr. Chairman, I don't really know. I am leaving now. When you have made the verification, please phone me at my office number and let me have your comments. Thank you for this opportunity".

Now I had to wait until the Chairman found out from the interpreters what they had heard, and all versions were corroborated. The only people who would not understand my speech, or Latin, would be the interpreters, so that they could not influence the interpretation of what had been heard by the ten people. They could only interpret what the ten people told them in their own language. This might take a little time, as perhaps the recording of what I had said was played over and over to the various people to get the true version of my statement to them.

I was a little nervous. This would be a momentous occasion for me as well as the people who had heard me during the live transmission. Now all I had to do was to wait for his phone call, while getting on with my office work.

In the office, I waited for the phone call from the Chairman. I realised that once he had accepted the truth in my statements, I would have to take some days off work to set up the interview. I knew the phone call would come shortly. I could not concentrate on my work, so I stopped and thought about what I would need to do next. I took out a piece of paper from my drawer and started jotting down all that I could think of, trying to put my ideas in some sequential order. After what seemed like hours, the phone rang and instantly I knew that it was from the Chairman. In fact, looking at my watch, it had only been 25 minutes; from the time I reached my office. I picked up the phone.

"Hallo. Is that Mr. Dass?" he asked before I could even say hallo.

I answered in the affirmative.

"I have verified everything from the ten people. It seems unbelievable, but it worked as you had said it would. I am ready to take the matter further. I think that we should meet as soon as possible." "I need a couple of days to get things sorted out in my mind, to clear my work at the office and to talk to God before I can see you. I will contact you tomorrow afternoon to set up the date and time for the meeting" I said. "Thank you for listening to me at the beginning and giving me the chance to prove myself. I know you must have thought me crazy at the time, and yet you gave me the chance. I personally feel that God may have had something to do with your decision."

I was now totally elated. Although I knew what happened would happen, it was still unbelievable and miraculous.

I went home that evening, thinking about everything I was going to tell God and about what I needed to ask Him. The interview would be some way off, but it was now definite.

That evening I talked to God and told Him all that had happened and that I now needed to meet the Chairman of the WCN to work out the logistics of setting the interview up so that all of mankind could tune in and hear what God had to say.

After having told God all my news, I said, "It is going to be very difficult for every human being to hear what You will say, as not everyone has the means of listening to broadcasts."

God said, "You go and do whatever is necessary. I will be with you all the way and will give you the words and ideas necessary to make it all possible. Tell them that I will take a human form at the interview. I also realise that the whole process will be a costly affair for the networks. I will allow advertisements and commercials to enable the costs to be met. It should, however, be made clear that only clean and safe adverts will be permitted, and I would need to know and approve, through you, the advert material and format before they can be broadcast. Tell the people concerned that unless the advert material and contents are cleared and approved by you, they will not be seen or heard by anyone at all."

I realised that God had left everything up to me to set up the interview. He would, no doubt, help me if needed, but now I had to get things arranged.

The next day I went to my office and requested my employer for one week off from the following day. It was very short notice, but I convinced them of the importance of my request, without having to go into details. I then phoned the Chairman of the WCN.

"Hallo. This is Ravi Dass. Will it be possible for us to meet tomorrow?"

"Yes, tomorrow will be fine. The sooner our meeting takes place, the better. I will cancel all my appointments for tomorrow and the next few days in order to see you and discuss how and what needs to be done. Can you be at my office at 9 in the morning?"

"Yes," I said, "I will bring some sort of agenda to work on and hopefully, in the next few days, we can work out a process to start the ball rolling to achieve our goal."

After a few minutes I was talking to the Chairman's secretary. "Hallo, Sally, can you let me know where to come for the meeting with the Chairman? Now that I am going to meet him finally for the first time, can you tell me his name, which I still do not know?"

"Yes, of course, Mr. Dass. The Chairman's name is Sir Roger Winthorpe."

The secretary gave instructions on how to get to the WCN offices.

That evening, I prepared, as best as I could, for the meeting with Sir Roger. A great deal would be ad hoc, thought out and discussed at the time of the meeting only. During the discussions, a great number of ideas and thoughts would surely present themselves.

I talked to God that evening and told Him of my meeting with Sir Roger the next morning and my preparations for the meeting. I asked for His blessings for the task ahead.

I slept soundly and woke up the next morning fully refreshed and raring to go. I had a light breakfast and a strong cup of coffee before leaving home.

It took me an hour and a half to reach the WCN offices, mainly due to the rush hour and traffic, but I was well in time for the appointment. I went inside the building and approached the reception desk in the hall.

"Good morning," I said. "My name is Ravi Dass and I have an appointment at 9 with Sir Roger Winthorpe, the Chairman."

The receptionist was expecting me. She said, "Please wait a few minutes while I speak with Sir Roger's secretary."

"This is Penny, at reception. I have Mr. Dass here for his appointment with Sir Roger. Shall I send him up now?"

Obviously, the answer was in the affirmative as Penny said, "Mr. Dass, please take the lift to the top floor, where Sir Roger's secretary will meet you."

I walked across to the lifts doors and pressed the button. As soon as the lift arrived, I got in and pressed the button for the top floor.

When the lift opened, I saw a middle-aged lady waiting. She smiled and said, "Hallo, Mr. Dass, my name is Sally Burgess. Nice to meet you in person at last. Sir Roger is waiting for you in his office. Please come this way."

Sally Burgess led me into a wide corridor, at the end of which was an ornate door. Through this was the room Sir Roger occupied as his office. She ushered me into the room and said, "Sir Roger, this is Mr. Dass." Sir Roger got up from behind his desk, came around to the front and extended his hand saying, "Good to meet you finally, Mr. Dass. You have certainly got my interest and my undivided attention. Please take a seat." He led me to an area towards the side of the room, where there was a coffee table and some comfortable armchairs.

He then turned to his secretary and said, "Sally, will you please bring us coffee?" Then he looked at me and asked, "Or would you like tea?"

"Coffee will be fine, Sir Roger," I said.

The secretary asked me, "How many lumps of sugar do you take in your coffee, Mr. Dass?"

I replied, "No sugar, thank you. I keep my own sweeteners with me."

Sally left and I turned towards Sir Roger, quite excited about the talks to follow. It hit me that finally things would start happening and that the coming interview with God was only a formality. It was the will of God. Everything would progress smoothly, and all necessary arrangements would be made without trouble.

Sir Roger looked at me intently and said, "Where do we start? Perhaps you might first tell me how this all came about."

I explained to Sir Roger how God had seemed to talk to me and how I had been skeptical about this at first. But after this had happened several times, I was convinced that God had actually spoken to me. I told everything about what God had asked me to do for Him and how it should be done. God would help me in convincing the media people and the people on earth that it was really He who would be speaking to them. This was the time when, after a little thought and research, that I contacted the WCN and had spoken to Sir Roger.

I explained that it would have been next to impossible for me to have got through to him and spoken to him the very first time I had tried calling him, unless God had a hand in it.

Sir Roger interrupted me at this point. "What you had stated to my secretary was extraordinary and really unbelievable, but obviously something made her talk to me about it. I was also impelled, by some unknown force to take it seriously and give you the chance to prove yourself. It now seems obvious to me that something beyond my comprehension was guiding our actions and responses."

I agreed with him wholeheartedly. "Sir Roger," I said, "the first thing that will need to be done is to contact all major TV and radio networks throughout the world and convince them of the need for their involvement, as this is necessary to reach out to all people on the planet. Only you can do this as you are held in high esteem throughout the world in the broadcast industry. You have been witness to a miraculous demonstration that has convinced you. Now you will have to convince all the others. I am sure that you will be able to do this."

"I agree with you, Ravi," said Sir Roger. "I hope you do not mind addressing you like this informally? Before we continue any further, please call me Roger. No formalities please, as we are going to be working close together for some time."

"OK, Roger, and thank you," I said. "Once you have convinced the other networks as to what is required from them, we will need to advertise this comprehensively throughout the world and also convince people to watch and hear the broadcast. We will need to ask them to send in questions that they want to ask of God. These will have to be sorted out, as many of the questions will be similar. Also, frivolous questions will have to be weeded out. At the end of the day, I do not expect much more than a handful of universal questions of any meaningful nature."

Sir Roger said, "All this is going to cost a great deal of money. I now totally believe in what we are about to do, and I am willing to utilise the WCN resources without thought of money. The WCN does not use advertising to obtain revenue; it gets its funding from the Government, through TV licences. But I am not sure that other networks would be willing or able to do the same."

"God has already thought about this problem. He had said that the networks can finance their costs through advertisements, but such advertisements should be clean and ones that do not cause harm to people who see or hear them. These adverts will have to be cleared through me, after my consultation with God. Any adverts that are not cleared will not be seen or heard by anyone, regardless of anyone trying to pull a fast one."

"That's a relief, because now it will be easier to convince the heads of various networks about what they are required to do. As we want the broadcast to be heard by everyone on earth, it would be necessary to set up large TV screens, loudspeakers and the like to cover places that have no TV or radio coverage in the remotest areas. This is where heavy costs are going to be incurred. Perhaps we can persuade various governments to assist in the finance of these, as in the long run these would be beneficial for any mass communication within the various countries."

The meeting went along in this vein and lasted through the day, broken for a quick lunch and periodic tea and coffee.

At the end of the day we had agreed on several ideas and decided to meet again in two days' time to discuss the initial responses from those who were being asked to get involved. We could then think about our next step and decide on a time span before we could actually have the interview.

Now that things seemed to be progressing in the manner hoped, I was relieved and more confident in the ultimate outcome. I was sure that Roger would be successful in convincing all the required people. He was a very highly respected person in his field and well regarded.

I went home in a very good and happy frame of mind. I told my wife and children what had taken place during the day. They were updated daily on the events of the day and had full knowledge about what was happening. They were fully supportive, happy in the knowledge that this was giving me good relief from my family problems as well as giving me confidence that such problems would sort themselves out in due course.

I talked to God that evening, as I did everyday, and gave Him all the details of what had been done during the day and the progress we had made. He was of course aware of everything, but it gave me peace and tranquility to talk to Him. I went to sleep that night in a calm frame of mind, away from all worries and problems.

The next morning, I woke up fully refreshed and looking forward to the task for the day, which was to research into the major religions in this world – from where they originated, what was their present following and teachings and, if possible, to find out if any fundamental changes had been made to their original Scriptures. This last piece of information would be the most difficult to find, if at all possible. Perhaps I would have to ask God!

I set about my task with vigour and zeal. I logged on into my computer and found my CD of the complete Encyclopedia Britannica, where I hoped I would find some useful information about the various religions. If this did not give me the information I sought, I would go on the internet and see what I could learn from there. It promised to be an arduous but exciting journey into the quest for religious knowledge.

I did not expect to delve too deeply into the information that might be available, but just enough so as to be able to deal with any queries, questions or criticisms from the various religious sects. At least I should be able to relate to their basic teachings and ideology.

I spent a considerable time getting the information and trying to digest it at the same time. I now felt that I was somewhat equipped to the challenge that I knew would be thrown at me. I then went through my list of things that had to be done and ticked off the items already dealt with. I also added items that came to mind, not listed before. This would be a continuing process until everything had been set and arranged.

That night, I went to sleep in anticipation of my meeting with Roger the next day and the news from him about what he had been able to achieve.

The next morning, I got ready and left home well in time to meet Roger at his office by 9, the time we had arranged to meet. This time, on reaching the reception, I was told to go straight to the top floor as Roger was expecting me.

Roger's secretary met me outside the lift saying, "Good morning Mr. Dass, Sir Roger is waiting for you in his room. Would you like for me to bring you coffee or tea?"

I said, "Tea would be fine, but no sugar."

I walked into Roger's office. He was sitting behind his desk. As soon as he saw me, he got up, came around and shook my hand, saying, "Good morning, Ravi. I have good news for you."

"Good morning, Roger," I said. "I expected good news as this is God's work, but nevertheless it is good to know that things are going according to plan."

"Let us wait for Sally to bring in the beverages and then I will update you on what has been happening in the last 24 hours."

Within a few minutes, Sally came in with coffee for Roger and tea for me. She placed these on the coffee table along with a plate of biscuits.

We sipped our drinks and Roger started the conversation. "I talked to the heads of the major TV networks and radio networks throughout the world yesterday. I had to start very early in the morning considering the time zone differences. I was able to get through to all the people, either at their homes or their offices. The last call was made at 10.30 last night." He paused for a few seconds before continuing, "I was able to convince all of them about the genuineness of the proposal. I told them about the evidence you had given to support your statements and how this had been verified to my complete satisfaction. As I was convinced with the evidence given, they were totally willing to accept it."

At this point I could not keep the excitement out of my voice. "This is fantastic, Roger. It is your standing and reputation that has made this possible so quickly and, of course, the help of God."

"More to do with the help from God. My relations with the various heads may also have helped a little," Roger said with a smile. "We also discussed various matters, including set up of large TV screens, loudspeakers etc., and also about how all the costs could be met."

He paused and took a sip of water from a glass before continuing. "They will get in touch with smaller networks in their areas, as I would also do, to explain and convince them of their roles. It was also felt that the various governments of the world had to be involved, not only for funding purposes but also to help out with the logistics of the operation. All the network bosses have agreed that any shortfall in funding could be met. With the enormity of the situation, advertising income would probably cover all costs and, more than likely, would net them a good profit as adverts placed during this period would be to the size of an audience never before imagined. So, the charge for such adverts would probably go through the roof."

I was astounded with what had been achieved in the very short space of time since our last meeting, two days ago. It seemed hardly possible, and I said so to Roger.

Roger responded, "I also find it hard to fathom that so much has been achieved so soon. Not only this, they will all come back to me regarding how to convey the interview proposal to the people as well as to collect the questions that people want to ask God. A great number of personnel will be involved. They are extremely excited about the whole thing. Certainly, this whole concept has resulted in greater cooperation between world networks than ever has been possible in the past and bodes well for the future, in network cooperation as well as for important worldwide issues. This is the ultimate as far as total communication is concerned. Nothing like this has ever been attempted nor is ever likely to be attempted in the future."

I too caught the excitement bug. "We need to give the whole thing some time to reach a satisfactory stage before the interview. When you hear anything which requires further action, please let me know immediately."

We said our goodbyes and I left for home.

It was now in the hands of Roger. He would be getting all the information and facts together for us to work on. Until such time I would carry on working. When the time came to take further leave, I would tell my employer the full story and of the necessity for my leave at such short notice once again. I think my employer at least deserved that. After knowing what I was involved in, I am sure they would be more than happy to cooperate.

Now that so much had happened and the outcome of the arrangements was a certainty, having to wait was agonising. It was extremely hard to concentrate on my work at the office. But it was unfair to my employer for me to lose concentration like this, so I made all efforts to work diligently and make sure that the work was done in time and did not suffer due to my thoughts on the coming interview with God.

I had hoped that busying myself with my office work would pass the time quicker, but this was not the case. The moments seemed to drag. It was not really a short period of time, but considering the enormity of the task in hand, the three weeks it took before Sir Roger contacted me was not too long either.

In the meantime, I had explained to my employer what was happening and why I would need to take holiday leave at very short notice. At first, they were very skeptical about what I had told them.

I did not expect anything less. I told them all that had happened and asked them to telephone Sir Roger to confirm what they had heard from me.

Their conversation with Roger convinced them fully. In fact, they were very generous and told me that I need not take any annual leave for this purpose. They were willing to give me paid leave for as long as required, to finish the task at hand.

I was very thankful to them and informed them that I would come into the office whenever I was not involved with the work given to me by God, perhaps a few hours or half a day here and there. They were happy with this arrangement.

When finally, Roger telephoned me I was just about to leave for home from my workplace.

"Hallo, Ravi, this is Roger. I have been in contact with all the people involved with the task at hand and have finalised a great many things, which I am sure you would find satisfactory." There was a slight pause and then he said, "Can you come in tomorrow morning? I think that we are at a stage now when we can really start to finalise and prepare for the interview and maybe even set a tentative date for it."

Before I could reply, Roger continued, "Have you sorted out your leave from work? We may need a week or two of intense preparations to fully finalise all the issues involved."

"Yes, Roger," I replied. "My employers have been very considerate and have given me leave for as long as I require. I will come to meet you in your office tomorrow. What time would you like me to meet you?"

"I am expecting a few more details by fax and some phone calls tomorrow morning, so perhaps you might like to come over at lunchtime. Let us have lunch together, when we can discuss things generally before going into details back at the office."

"Do you want me to come into the office or meet you at the place where we are to have lunch?"

"Come into the office first and from there we will go to the restaurant together. There is a very nice little restaurant near here that is not only quiet but serves excellent food. Let us meet at 12.30." I went home that night and related all that had happened during the day to my family. They often pitched in with a number of ideas about what should be done and how. All this was very invaluable to me for the task ahead.

I got up early so that I could collect my thoughts about what needed to be discussed with Roger that afternoon. I noted down all the points that had been suggested to me by my family and some that I had thought of myself. I was now prepared to meet Roger and hoped to have things moving to a final conclusion before the day was over. I have a habit of being punctual and I reached Roger's office at exactly 12.30 in the afternoon. Roger was ready and we went out almost immediately. We walked a few blocks from his office into a quiet cul-desac. There was a small and cosy French restaurant at the end, which was obviously very popular, as it was quite full. Roger had booked a table for us, and we were ushered in. Our table was in a booth, giving us privacy as well as relative quietness. From the attention given to Roger and the location of the table, it seemed that he was a frequent and valued customer at the restaurant.

We sat down at the table and Roger asked me, "What would you like to drink?"

I replied, "I feel that my head should be clear for what lies ahead, so I will have a fresh orange juice, thank you."

Roger said to the waiter, "Bring us two freshly squeezed orange juices, please. We will order lunch in a little while."

As the waiter left, Roger said, "I will dispense with any starters and have only the main meal, as too heavy a lunch and a full stomach would not allow me to fully concentrate on the task ahead."

I agreed with Roger and told him that this was exactly what I had also decided. A light lunch would allow us to concentrate better on the matters in hand.

Roger recommended breast of chicken stuffed with spinach with sautéed potatoes and a salad.

The waiter arrived with our orange juice. We ordered our meal, asking that it should be ready not before 30 minutes, as we wanted to discuss a few things before the meal. When the waiter left with our order, Roger said, "I received the various phone calls and faxes that were expected this morning. They have now set in motion the next and possibly the final stages of the task in hand."

I asked, "How far have you got with the various networks and other people involved, in setting up the conditions necessary for the interview?"

"I have been assured that all networks, both TV and radio, as well as all governments concerned, have agreed to collectively co-ordinate the relay of the broadcast so that everyone is able to hear or watch it live. TV screens and loudspeakers are being put in place for the broadcast. Satellite systems are being set up and coordinated for the event. The costing and funding are being worked out and the various governments have agreed to help towards covering costs."

"What about informing all the people about the coming interview? What is being done, so that they become aware and look out for the date of the interview yet to be announced?"

"TV, radio and newspaper advertisements will appear on a regular basis, informing people about this. Also, leaflets are to be dropped in areas where TV and radio broadcasts are not the norm. Governments have organised personnel to go out to the remote areas and personally inform people of this. They will also be told of the miracle being performed in order for them to understand what is being said."

"Any response regarding questions people want to ask God at the interview?" I asked.

"Yes", answered Roger. "At present they are collecting the responses and will give us a list of the relevant questions as soon as they have sorted them out."

"I had talked to God and had asked Him about the time differences throughout the world and how this would affect the broadcast," I said. "He told me that He would have to perform another miracle. The broadcast would be heard throughout the world at exactly the same time. That is to say that if we broadcast it at 12 noon, then it will also be heard by everyone in their own countries at 12 noon their time. The laws of time will be suspended during the broadcast but will revert back to normal after the broadcast. This will mean that at the time of the broadcast, no one will be asleep or tired. The mind boggles at this. It is almost impossible to comprehend. If anyone has any doubts, this miracle will convince them."

Roger was astonished at what I had just stated. "Wow, this is something! When the time comes for setting the date of the interview, we will have to include this in informing people of the broadcast date." "Another thing, Roger," I said. "The interview will take place without any live audience, with only absolutely necessary technical personnel, plus our immediate family members, in a small room as appropriate for the occasion. This is what is required by God."

"Where would the interview take place?" Roger asked.

"As everything is being organised through you, Roger, the ideal place would be at an appropriate WCN studio."

"I don't think that anyone will begrudge the WCN in this matter," Roger said.

By this time our lunch had arrived. It looked very appetising and delicious. We ate in silence, enjoying the food and also thinking about what we had just discussed. After the meal we finished with a cup of coffee.

Roger insisted on paying the bill after which we left for his office to continue our talks. Once we had reached the office, we sat down and worked out what we should do during the rest of the day.

It was decided that we would contact all the people we had been in touch with before, to let them know about what we had discussed at lunch, about the interview and to look out for the interview date to be announced. We would also tell them about the miracle of the timing of the broadcast.

Roger phoned all the networks and informed everyone. He also asked them to let him have the final list of questions to be asked of God during the interview as soon as they were ready. Finally, Roger asked them to let him have a tentative date for the interview. Once the final program and all such dates were known, we would be able to make a decision regarding the actual final date.

All this took us the rest of the afternoon and well into the evening. At 9 in the evening, we finally finished.

We were told that they all would come back to us with the necessary information and finalisation of the program within a week, at which point we would be able to set an actual date for the interview.

I did, however, ask for the questions that they had received to be given to me as soon as possible. I was informed that these would be faxed to Roger once they had all been collated, which would not take more than 2 to 3 days. I asked Roger to keep me informed and let me know as soon he got them.

I left the WCN offices at 9.15 in the evening, arriving home much later than normal. All members of my family were awake, waiting to hear what progress had been made. I told them of the events of the day and informed that the interview would be held soon. They were all very excited and hoped that everything would be finalised in a satisfactory manner soon.

It was rather late when I went to sleep, as I had to talk to God first, giving Him the news about the events during the day.

The next morning, I got up a little later than usual. I decided to go to work, as there was nothing I could do until Roger contacted me.

At my workplace, I was asked to meet my manager in his room. I went in to see him.

On entering his room, he asked me to sit down and enquired about the progress with the project relating to the interview with God. I filled him in with all the information to date and told him that I could come in to work for a few days and that Roger would contact me when I was required.

I also told him that things were moving and that the time was approaching when the interview would be taking place.

He wished me well and said that he was looking forward to listening and seeing the interview.

For the next couple of days, I went to work as usual and tried to concentrate on work in my office. I made sure that I only started work that I could complete at that point in time. I did not want to leave anything partly done. Other people could take on new work while I was away.

A few days later I received a call from Roger informing me that he had received a fax listing the questions to be asked of God. I told him that I would come into the office next morning and go through the list. I would decide which questions should be asked at the interview after talking to God.

After completing the day's work in the office, I informed my manager that I would now be away from work for longer than before as the time was approaching for the interview.

The next morning, I went to the WCN offices to see Roger. On reaching the top floor, Sally took me straight into Roger's office.

Roger was seated behind his desk and smiled when he saw me. He had a piece of paper in his hand that he had been looking at when I entered; he got up from his desk and came round to shake my hand, saying, "Good morning, Ravi. I have the list of questions to ask God at the interview. They have been sorted to represent the main theme of questions received from various people throughout the world. The questions are fairly similar, so the list of questions is not too long." He gave me the list and added, "The people sorting the list seem to have done a good job, as the list is fairly representative of the type of questions one would like to ask God, and there seem to be no frivolous questions."

We went and sat down by the coffee table, where I looked at the sheet of paper in my hand. On reading all the questions, I realised that the questions listed were very similar to the kind of questions that I had thought of asking. Although the list was not long, it covered quite a vast area of answers being sought.

I discussed the list with Roger and we both agreed that the list was suitable and there was nothing more to be added.

Roger was expecting information in the next day or two to finalise the date and timing of the interview. He would contact me as soon as this had been decided.

That night I talked to God and informed Him of the list of questions that people wished to ask Him. He told me that He would address the people first before answering any questions. He said that a great many of the answers would automatically be evident in the talk he wanted to give. Any questions not covered by his talk would be dealt with at the end.

After telling me this God said, "Ravi, after the interview I would like you to travel around the world and meet people from all countries and walks of life. This would take a number of years. I want you to find out what effect my talk had on them. Did it open their eyes and alter their thinking and way of life for the better, or was it the case of in one ear and out the other? People seem to have short memories where their true welfare is concerned. You will have to follow up my talks and instill in people the necessity of changing their pattern of life if they want to be happy. A lot needs to be done before people forget what they will be told. I am sure that the WCN will be glad to fund such an exercise to incorporate into their TV programs as a sequel and follow-up of my talks. I will go into more detail regarding this trip with exactly what I want you to convey to everyone you come in contact with during the trip, at a later stage, once the interview has been organised."

I thought about what God had just said. I understood the reason behind God's wishes. By experience I knew how easily people tend to forget, where it involved any amount of effort on their part to do the things necessary for their own good. Generally, people tend to take the easy path, unless it was pressed home to them time and time again. Perhaps this was the purpose of the trip around the world God wanted me to take, which in my view, was certainly needed.

I would discuss this with Roger, the next time I met him. I was sure that the phenomenal coverage of God's interview, and the interest it would create, would result in many follow-ups. It would be lucrative for the networks. The funding for my travels would not be difficult. I hoped to be able to take my wife with me on the travels, to help in this regard.

The next couple of days were spent in getting prepared for the interview. I started thinking about how to best approach this and how to introduce it on TV.

I felt that Roger should introduce the program, as he was in full knowledge of what was going on. As a result of the total conviction that Roger had, the introduction would carry a great deal of weight and would make people want to listen to the broadcast. Any other person doing the introduction to the broadcast would not be suitable as most people would be skeptical initially, and this would not carry the conviction necessary for people to listen to every word of the broadcast.

A few days later, Roger telephoned me to let me know that everyone was now fully aware of the interview that was due to take place. The date had been set for 4 weeks later, on a Saturday at precisely 12 noon, London time. Of course, the time throughout the world would be different but would register as 12 noon on the same day, as promised by God.

There now did not seem much for me to do until the time came for the interview, but I wanted to see where the interview would take place and asked Roger to show me the final arrangements regarding the interview so that changes, where necessary, could be made in time without any problem. Roger told me that he would phone me in a few days' time, once the venue had been set.

It was necessary to get the place and background for the interview just right. It should be simple but elegant, not showy in any way whatsoever.

I went back to my workplace, to carry on my normal duties awaiting the phone call from Roger, when I would take some time off to see the arrangements for the interview. Then I could continue doing my office work and wait for the day of the interview.

A couple of days later my phone rang.

It was Roger. "Good morning, Ravi. We have finalised the venue of the broadcast. Perhaps you would come in tomorrow and look the place over. I can also fill you in on other matters which have now been fully completed or will be completed well before the date of the interview."

I thanked Roger and said, "Roger, apart from what you have just stated I need to discuss something else with you. After the interview God has asked that I do a sort of follow-up to the interview, for which I will need your help and guidance. I will give you the details when I see you tomorrow."

We agreed to meet the next day in his office at 10 in the morning. Roger must have wondered as to what I wanted to discuss with him the next day, but I felt that it was not something I could tell him on the phone. He was too much of a professional to press me any further.

The next morning, I arrived at the WCN offices a few minutes early and was ushered into Roger's office immediately.

Roger greeted me, "Hallo, Ravi, good to see you. Before going to see the venue and arrangements for the interview, let me bring you up to date with all that has been or will be arranged by various networks and agencies well before the date of the interview. Also, we can discuss what you wanted to talk to me about this morning."

We were facing each other across his desk.

Roger continued, "I have been informed that full advertising through media, newspapers, distribution of pamphlets, word of mouth and every other conceivable method will start from tomorrow so that all people are fully aware of the date and time of the interview. The people will also be made aware of the miracles being performed at the interview stage to bring this coverage to them in order to convince them of the genuineness of what is going to happen. All commercial and private airlines, shipping and fishing vessels, trains, coaches and all other forms of group travel are being directed to install communication devices so that they can listen and or see the interview. Anyone not able to do this will be told to put their journey on hold until the broadcast has ended. Arrangements are being made to cover the broadcast at places like hospitals, prisons, hostels, etc. Everyone will be told to make sure that they keep themselves free during the broadcast. All activities should be left until after the broadcast. No stone is being left unturned to achieve a 100% audience."

I was impressed with what Roger had just told me. I could imagine the immense work and effort that all this involved. In fact, at this point a thought crossed my mind. If all this could be mobilised in a reasonably short period of time, why can't such efforts be made for betterment of the world, at frequent intervals? I needed to think about this in depth and look at the possibilities.

I said, "Roger, what you tell me is tantamount to a minor miracle being performed by man, although perhaps with a little help from God."

Roger smiled at this.

I continued, "About what I wanted to discuss with you today, God has asked me to tour the world after the interview, meeting people from all countries and walks of life to find out what effect the message of God has had on them and how this would change their lives and habits, if at all. God has told me to make sure that His message is kept alive in the minds and hearts of all people. They should not be allowed to forget what He will tell them, if they want to live a happy and satisfactory life."

Roger seemed interested in what I was telling him. Before he could say anything, I continued, "All this will cost money, as I will not be able to pay for this myself. God felt that such a project would create useful and lucrative sequels to the interview with Him. Both my wife and I would need to go together, as this might take a number of years to be effective. What do you think? Would the WCN be interested in funding this?" It was a direct question.

Roger did not take long to reply. "Ravi, I think it's a wonderful idea. We could have live coverage of your talks with various people and arrange TV coverage of synopses of your talks on a regular basis. We have our network spread all over the world, so arranging a TV crew to accompany you would not be difficult. I will work out the basis of this and when you are ready, I will make sure that you have all the necessary funding that is required. As we would be getting benefit of such programs for broadcasting, we will discuss a salary for you and your wife. Let me work on it."

I was happy with the way things were going. Now all I had to do was to wait for the day of the interview. I was certain that things would go smoothly. After all it was God's work.

After this we went to look at the venue and arrangements for the interview. Roger took me to the WCN studios.

Once we reached there, he took me to a room that had a small stage, plain and simple. There was seating for 8 people off the stage and enough space for three cameras, covering all angles of the stage.

Roger said, "This seems appropriate, as per your requirement. It is small, simple and has appropriate TV cameras for full coverage. I suggest that the space for seating be for your family and myself and my family, if you are agreeable. I am sure you have kept your family informed of whatever has been happening, as I have."

"I am sure that this will not present a problem," I said. "You will have to ward off requests for audience from any faction or media people. I am sure that you will be able to handle this."

Roger said, "I will see to it. It should not present a problem, as it is the wish of God not to have an audience in the studio. Perhaps you should also clear with God about our families being in the studio for the interview. Let me know if it is OK." Roger kept silent for a few minutes and then he cleared his throat and said, "Ravi, I would consider it an honour if you and your family could come and have dinner at my house, Saturday week at 8 in the evening. We have not known each other too long, but I think our relationship has progressed and we have become quite close. Certainly, I feel that way. I hope you feel the same way."

I was touched and said, "Roger, thank you for your kindness. Yes, I feel the same way too. I accept your kind hospitality on behalf of my family and myself. I hope it would not cause any inconvenience; my wife is a vegetarian."

"No, not at all. We will look forward to seeing you and your family soon."

Roger then gave me his address and instructions on how to get there and then we parted. If there was anything important, we would contact each other, otherwise we would meet up for dinner at his house. The next morning, I switched on the radio and also turned on the TV. Within 10 minutes I heard the announcement for the interview date along with the details of the miracles being performed.

The media had chosen an ideal person to announce on TV and the voice on the radio was also of the same person. The sincerity and belief with which the person made the announcement, made the message totally genuine and believable. I turned to other TV and radio channels and found that the same message was being relayed everywhere at various times. The broadcasts were frequent.

When I left for work, on reaching the railway station from where I took the train, I found leaflets with similar message regarding the interview. All the newspapers were also printing the message across their front page. Posters were placed all over giving the same information.

From what I saw, I was convinced that this was a pattern being repeated throughout the world.

There was no doubt in my mind, if there ever had been, of the thoroughness of the operation being carried out to inform everyone of the interview with God.

People from all over seemed to be talking about nothing else but this. The response and interest were immense, and I was certain it would be the same all over the world.

Every day people were being reminded and informed. By the time the date for the interview came around, there would not be a soul in the world who was not aware of the forthcoming interview.

I was certain that everyone in this world would hear the message of God.

Now that everything had been settled, the time waiting for the date for the interview seemed to drag for me. I just wanted time to fly.

On the day for dinner with Roger and his family, I arrived with my wife and my two children at Roger's home at 8 in the evening. I rang the bell.

Roger opened the door. I introduced my wife and children to him. He led us into his living room, where we saw an elegant lady and two young people, a woman and a man, whom I took to be his wife and children.

Once we were in the room, he introduced us to his wife and children. His wife's name was Elizabeth and his children's names were David and Jane.

After the introduction, we all sat down on the comfortable settees in the living room. He asked us what we would like to drink.

While he was getting us the drinks I said to Roger's wife, "Thank you for inviting us to dinner. I hope that you will allow us the honour of being your hosts in the very near future."

Elizabeth replied, "We would be delighted. This whole affair is very exciting. We have been talking about nothing else all this time. I only hope that people take notice of what God tells them and change their thoughts and way of life to make this world a better place for everyone to live in."

She paused as Roger came back with the drinks on a wheeled trolley.

He handed the drinks to everybody and raised his glass. "Cheers", he said. "Good health and happiness to all. I am certain that the world will change for the better after the broadcast. Let us hope that this time, people will pay heed to the message to be given by God and not keep on making the same mistakes they have been making throughout. I do not think that this opportunity will come again. If we do not make good use of this opportunity, then the world is doomed."

The young ones left the room, no doubt to talk about their own world, and the four of us were left in the living room.

We talked mainly about the topic of the moment, discussing the impact on people and whether they would be willing to make the effort to change the world into a better place. It required a great amount of sacrifice on the part of everyone. Would people be willing to give up their conveniences and interests for the common good on a prolonged and continuous basis? That was the sixty-four-thousand-dollar question!

I was hopeful for an initial positive response, but would this continue? People are extremely fickle and centred around their possessions and advantages. Would they be willing to give these up permanently?

During our discussions, Elizabeth left us to set the table for dinner. A short while later, she called us all into the dining room.

The dining room was large with a 12-seat dining table. The table was set beautifully, with steaming dishes of aromatic food.

We all sat down to a sumptuous meal. Elizabeth had taken a great deal of trouble in preparing the meal and everyone enjoyed it.

On finishing the meal, we all showed our appreciation by thanking her.

During the meal and afterwards when we were having coffee, we continued our talks. Everyone was now waiting for the day of the interview.

At about 11, we bid Roger and his family farewell, with our invitation to them for dinner at our house, a week after the interview. The evening had gone well, and we had made good friends. The children also had enjoyed themselves and had promised to keep in touch with each other.

We arrived home fairly late and being somewhat tired decided to call it a day and go to sleep. Before falling to sleep I talked to God and told Him about our evening with Roger and his family, and how we had all clicked and made lifelong friends.

The next day I woke up and got ready for work. It was now about a week before the interview date. I was expecting calls and comments from religious sources regarding the interview but had not been informed of any so far.

I did not expect to receive any directly as I had requested that my identity should be kept secret and out of public knowledge before the interview. I was not equipped to deal with a massive number of queries, whereas the networks had staff to handle this.

It was lucky that I had taken such precautions as later that afternoon Roger telephoned me to tell me that the studio had received letters and phone calls, angry about our claim of the interview with God. These were mainly from various clergy throughout the world.

Roger said, "I have arranged to send replies telling all to watch the TV broadcast before commenting on our claim and assure them that their questions will be answered by God during the broadcast. There are always going to be people who would be skeptical and unbelieving. Anyway, there is not much we can do, except hope that they all will realise the truth soon."

I agreed with Roger and knew that such comments and queries would be coming in at least until the time for the interview. After that, hopefully, the matters would be clarified to everyone's complete satisfaction. All persons dealing with phone calls and letters were told to make the same statement to all such people – wait until after the interview before making up their minds.

I discussed this with God that night and relayed to Him what had been arranged and suggested by Roger.

God said, "I think you should take this head on and make a statement to the clergy. Use the same method of convincing them as with the ten people at the beginning. Speak to them in Latin so that they will know that a miracle is indeed being performed. This way, the true believers would be calmed and receptive to the interview and will not deter people of their congregation from listening to the interview. This way the networks will not be hounded with such letters and phone calls to distract them from the more important work in hand. A few sceptics may remain, but then there will always be such people." "If that is your bidding, I will ask Roger to convey to the sceptics that I will give a statement to them in Latin."

The next day I contacted Roger and told him about the suggestion made by God and asked him to set up a worldwide radio broadcast for this purpose at 2 in the afternoon the next day in order for the clergy in question to listen to the broadcast.

I made notes on what I wanted to say and then waited to broadcast my statement, the next day.

At 1.45pm the next day, I was ushered into the WCN studio to give my statement over the WCN worldwide radio network.

At 2 precisely I started broadcasting my statement. Nam blandit Londino, et quidquid in mundi parte diei tempus est. Ut intelligeres te et erunt quae aguntur per voluntatem Dei. Loquar in English quamquam audies verba mea in Latin, nescio quo verbo a te signum eius quod probare Deum esse molestie perfecerat. Audies linguam Latinam in hoc quod sentient plenque non sciunt, sed in hoc sensu decipher lingua tua te intelligam. Post haec fieri probation quae uel dubia adhuc futurum, in culmen sermonis Dei. "Good afternoon from London, or whatever time of day it is in your part of the world. In order to convince you about what has been and will be happening by God's wishes, I will speak in English, although you will hear my statement in Latin, a word of which I do not know, a miracle being performed by God to convince you of His involvement. You will hear this statement in Latin, which most of you will not know, but your mind will decipher this in your own language. After this you should have no doubt as the genuineness of what has happened or yet to happen, culminating in the interview with God."

I hoped that my broadcast statement would now put to rest the angry outcry from the clergy of various religious beliefs and the work in hand could go ahead without any further distractions.

I talked to God every day until the day of the interview. He had told me that He would meet me at the interview venue a few minutes before the time of the broadcast. He would take an appropriate human form, and I would definitely recognise Him.

The day for the interview finally arrived without any more outcries of disbelief. I woke up with great emotion and expectations. I got ready, taking care that I was dressed in a neat and sober fashion befitting the occasion. My wife and children also got ready.

This was going to be the most momentous and important day not only of my life, but that of everyone else.

I left home a little earlier than normal. I wanted to get to the studios at least 30 minutes before the interview to check that the arrangements were satisfactory and also to talk to Roger.

I drove to the studios in silence, thinking about the day ahead. I noticed the lack of traffic and people on the roads. I assumed that people had already settled down to watch or listen to the broadcast. The few people hat I saw on the roads were probably on their way to places where they could listen to or watch the broadcast.

It was a brilliant day, sunny and very pleasant, as I had expected. I turned on my car radio and listened to the news. They were broadcasting details of the interview. The news also stated the weather conditions throughout the world. It was not surprising to note that the weather throughout the world was similar – fine and sunny. The weather broadcasters were saying how very unusual this was. The weather had never been identical, at the same time, everywhere in the world. It was another proof of the authenticity of the moment.

Due to the lack of traffic, I reached the studios a good 50 minutes before the interview. I parked the car near the entrance in the space that had been provided especially for me. Without this, it would have been difficult for me to park anywhere near the entrance to the building today.

I went into the building and was immediately surrounded by a number of the WCN staff, all asking questions regarding the interview and wishing me good luck. I answered whatever questions I could and thanked them for their good wishes.

I found my way to the studio where the interview was to take place and saw that Roger was already there, talking to one of the cameramen. His family were seated in front of the stage. I told my family to sit next to them. I left them all to talk to each other and turned towards where Roger was standing.

I walked up to him and said, "Hallo, Roger, the day and time has finally arrived. I expect you are as excited as I am. God has told me that He would be here a few minutes before the broadcast, in a human form. He told me that I would be able to recognise that it was Him."

I looked at Roger's face. He could not hide his excitement; his face was totally animated.

I asked, "Have you got your introduction prepared and ready?"

He said, "Yes, I have been working on how I should make the introduction. I think I have got it as appropriate as the occasion demands."

Roger then turned to the cameramen and asked, "Is everything set up for the interview?"

They all assured him that they were fully prepared and ready.

By this stage, considerable time had elapsed and before we knew it, the time for the broadcast had nearly come.

I suddenly realised it was time that God had said He would be here.

I looked around and saw a kindly looking gentleman of approximately 60, with a radiant face, standing by the chairs on the stage.

I caught my breath, and, in that instant, everyone realised that God was here, and all eyes turned to look at Him.

Everyone who was seated got up and bowed as well as all those that were standing. We all felt His radiance and goodness engulf us.

There was tranquility and peace in the atmosphere the likes of which I had never witnessed before.

Everyone felt privileged to be in the presence of God. I suddenly realised that we were indeed singled out to be privileged, as all other human beings would only see Him on TV or hear Him on radio. We were the only people who were seeing Him, in person, by our side. All our lives had suddenly changed. We would not be the same we were a few moments ago.

I went over to where God was standing and knelt down before Him. He put his hands around me and pulled me to my feet, saying, "We finally meet in person. All of you have done a good job in setting this up. I believe the time has arrived for the broadcast to go on air. I know that all the people present here want to talk to me. I will talk to all after the broadcast."

I managed to say, "Yes, Sir, please be seated."

At this point, the chief cameraman said, "Please take your places, as we are due to go on air in exactly two minutes."

Roger was standing by the side of the stage, from where he would give the introduction, after which he would go and sit down next to his family, in front and below the stage.

I was sitting in one of the two chairs on the stage facing the chair on which God was seated.

A red light indicated that there was 10 seconds to go for the start of the program; after 10 seconds a green light came on and the cameras focused on Roger.

"It is our privilege to be in the position to broadcast this historic interview with God. You have all been made aware of how this will be heard and seen by you in all corners of the world at the same time. You will surely be aware that this can only be possible through a miracle performed by God." Roger paused to look directly into the camera and continued, "God is appearing in a human form to be interviewed by Ravi Dass. The questions you were asked to send, have been reduced to 4 or 5 that cover everything that you wanted to know. Before God answers the questions, He will address you. Most of the answers to the questions asked will, in all likelihood, be answered by what He wants to say to all of us. There is no need for me to introduce you, as you will all know, immediately, who is who." Roger paused and then turning towards the stage. "I hand you over to Ravi Dass."

With this he swiftly and quietly moved down to where he was to be seated, next to his family.

CHAPTER 5

The Audience

The camera focused on me. "Sir, people throughout the world are anxiously waiting to listen to what You have to say." God adjusted his position on the chair and looked straight at the camera which was now turned towards Him.

"All you people are, no doubt, astonished at seeing and hearing me, wondering what caused me to come amongst you. Firstly, I want to talk about what you call religion. A number of preachers and clerics of all religions are sincere and dedicated people, of that I am certain. But it seems that some are confused, whilst others have a different view of me, than should be the case. Let me explain.

From the outset, let me say that religion should not be made into an industry where certain religious leaders and clerics are using religion for their own purposes, to feather their nests and to gain publicity for their own selfish ends. I do not condone such actions, nor do I regard these people as having any right to spread my message. There are a number of such people all over the world, who take advantage of you and your desire to get nearer to me. Use your judgement. Do not be fooled by such people. No one who is my disciple will want to accumulate wealth or live in the luxury that some of these people do. They seem to have no humility. Power, in my name, has gone to their head.

Unfortunately, the selfish desires of such people are advanced by the public itself. In certain countries the public wrongly put such clerics on a pedestal, who then get into political camps that try to woo them to get the vote of their followers, without realising the harm they are doing. They think of God only when they want to get votes. There are others who are not politically minded as such, but who use popularity with their followers to create importance for themselves and thereby are able to live in luxury and amass wealth. It is not right for clerics to live in such style or to command such wrong influence over people. They create unhealthy differences and problems to achieve their ends. The public should see into the wrong doings of such people and not give them support. They do not deserve it.

Religious preachers and clerics should be concerned only with spreading my word, not indulging in politics, power or avarice. All religious teachings and tenets are directly linked to me. Just as I have come down in the form of Jesus Christ to people of Christian beliefs, I have also manifested as Brahma, Vishnu and Shiva in the Hindu faith; I am Allah revealed by the Prophet Muhammad to people on earth in the Islamic belief of Muslims; Sikhism believes in the Supreme Being, the one and only God; Buddhists do not worship me as God but they strive for a deep insight into the true nature of life focusing on personal development which is the same as following my teachings and word. The people who follow Jainism and the teaching of Sai Baba are all following me. All religions have the same principles of how to live life in the correct manner.

I am One, not different to different religions, but incorporated into their beliefs in one way or another to live the kind of life that

I advocate. I have manifested myself to different people in different ways to consider their different cultures etc., so that they are able to understand what I have to say. All religions are basically about me and my teachings to mankind. If you understand this basic fact, then you will realise that different religions do not present any dangers to each other. They should complement each other. In fact, there should be togetherness amongst all religions. This does not appear to be the case. There are animosities, quarrels and competition amongst religions. This, perhaps, has to do with interpretation of the Scriptures over the years. The interpretation seems to have changed my basic teachings. It is time that all people who believe in me start to think clearly and deeply about what I teach.

It is wrong for you to change my teachings. A number of people are taking advantage of their own interpretation to do things in my name that I do not at all condone. Violence and killings are being carried out in my name, and people are made to believe that such deeds are for my sake and sanctioned by me. To the people who are carrying out such vile deeds, I would say for them to stop, as this is evil and has nothing to do with me. There is no excuse for taking innocent lives under any circumstances. If there is to be any fighting, this should be a fight against evil forces. Evil forces are those that try to take you away from my teachings and from that which is good. Evil forces are those that tempt you to harm others for your own personal interests and benefits. There are such evil forces which are inherent in all of you. You should individually fight these evil forces within you. If you do this then the need for fighting each other will disappear. All acts of violence that you commit are because of the devil within you, not as a result of the action of other people. You allow yourselves to be carried away by the action of others without really questioning your own motives or why the other person felt impelled to do what they did. If you try to put yourselves in the shoes of the other person, it will be possible to find peaceful solutions without having to resort to violent means. If you are reasonable and give due consideration to the feelings and problems of other people and not solely think of your own selves then you will realise that your problems are, perhaps, not so great. You will be able to relate to the rest of the world and your fellow human beings, making it easier to deal with any problems that today seem to result in a crisis everywhere.

This is the message I want to give the preachers and clerics who are my messengers. All of you should be concerned with unifying mankind through religious beliefs and trying to drive out the devil within, and not trying to inflame the differences that exist, but highlighting the common areas of the various religions. This would be a more profitable area to concentrate on, to create a unified and better world; this process of tolerance, unity and understanding should be applied in every sphere of human activity to allow peaceful ways to solve world problems. Anger, intolerance, lack of understanding and lack of unity will not solve the problems of your world. To all people, I stress the need to make changes for the better through peaceful means; by using the power you have in numbers, in choosing the right leaders to govern you. You can stop the wrong actions of your leaders and to make them seek peaceful means to end disputes. To do this, ego and self interest have to be forsaken. Interest of all should be considered in relation to what is right and practical. What is right and what is wrong? I have given all of you the means to comprehend whether what you do is right or wrong. This is through your conscience. When you do something, your conscience automatically tells you whether it is right or wrong. Many a times, despite knowing what you are doing is wrong, you carry on doing it. You should let your conscience be a guide when you are unsure. You should not do wrong things, even if seems expedient at the time. It is very difficult to undo wrong doings. Do the right thing at all times. In the long run it will be beneficial for you. Do not always take the easy path. This will inevitably lead you to difficulties in the long term, however comfortable it may be in the short term. It will not last and will have a bad effect for a long time.

It has been a very long time since I was amongst you and told you the way that you should all live your lives. What I gave you were the basic laws for a satisfactory life. The ultimate choice was yours. It has become apparent that the choices you have made are leading you to destroy your own world. I have come to make you all realise that you will have to make great changes in your way of thinking, way of living, and dealing with and relating to each other, if you are to avert the impending disaster to your world. You are too concerned with self-interest in the narrow sense of the word. If you consider the same self-interest in the universal sense, you will realise that your interests are intertwined and dependent on living harmoniously with each other.

Before I expand on this, let me tell you that you all have a choice as to how you want to live your life. Your life is not predetermined. I do not know what will happen to you in the future. You may consider what I have just said as odd, as you believe that I know everything, and therefore how can your future be of your own making? Yes, I have the power to know about your future also, but I have taken this power away from myself and instead have given you the power over your own destiny. Your destiny depends totally on what you do and how you live your life. You have no fallback on me. It is entirely in your hands. Although I do not know what will happen to you for sure since I have discarded this power, common sense tells me that the course you are following can only lead to destruction. If you think clearly, you too will realise that this is so.

In saying all this I am trying to awake in all of you the responsibility for safeguarding your world, by doing what is right. You know what is necessary, but you do not know what to do. The importance you give to your own narrow interests, ambitions and greed do not allow you to progress towards creating a better world for everyone. You are so engrossed in the pursuit of material possession, comforts and easy living, that to give importance to creating a better world would mean heavy sacrifices that are difficult for you to make. Some of you may think that you are well off and quite comfortable and you are in no way affected by what is happening around you, but this would be wrong because things are not static. They can change very quickly unless all of you do something about directing the changes for the better and not allowing changes to be thrust upon you that are detrimental in safeguarding your world.

You have a duty to care about each other and this can only happen if you are truly concerned about the plight of others. There are limited resources in this world and if you take out more than you need and waste them through useless and meaningless utilisation, you are only depriving other people the use of such assets, thereby directly causing them harm. Everyone has the right to live a comfortable life, but not to the extent that some people do. Everyone should get their worldly rewards in relation to the efforts they put in, but I see that the rewards, in many cases, are completely out of proportion to the efforts put in by some. These people are born with natural gifts, for example in terms of artistic nature or in other fields. These gifts, that I have given, are to enhance the quality of life in the world. The benefits gained through these natural gifts are not achieved through any great effort by the persons concerned. Why then should these people expect and take out from the system far, far more than they themselves have put in? The fact that people with such gifts are a rarity only means that value is added to the lives of other people and because of this, these gifted people should take a little more than other 'ordinary' people out of the system, but certainly not the immensely vast amounts that they demand for themselves. The price paid for their product would be cheaper, if amounts demanded by such people were reasonable, thereby giving more people access to the products at an affordable cost and benefiting all. The excesses claimed by such people only deny other people their share for even a very basic living. This is wrong. This is one of the reasons why so much turmoil exists in the world, which is part of the cause that can lead to its destruction. The fault mainly lies with the general public. You give too much importance to such people and place them on a pedestal making them feel that they are special and that they have a right to take out more from the system than they deserve. They are special only because you make them special. They should not take such a vast advantage of this. They must be more down to earth and keep their feet on the ground.

I am not advocating the communist system. I am just saying that genuine efforts of people should be rewarded. Gifted people give a great deal of happiness and pleasure to others and therefore deserve somewhat more from their efforts than perhaps others. Easy and vast rewards for minor efforts should not be demanded by such people. Hard work and enterprise should be rewarded as with other good traits, but in a fair manner, after considering the rarity factor which may allow somewhat more but fair excesses.

This is all in your own hands. If you allow this to happen then you should not complain about the problems that ensue. You can only take out what is available and if you wrongly give this to people who do not necessarily deserve it, then you are depriving others, including yourself, a fair share of the assets available in the system. This is applicable to individuals as well as nations.

Strong people have a duty to help and protect the weaker sections of society, not taking everything for themselves, but to utilise their strength to help others to make this a better and more liveable world. Perhaps I am advocating Utopia, but this is not impossible. All it requires is a little less greed on your part. If everyone is a little less greedy, then the world can change for the better.

When you start acting on this, you will realise that life is more wonderful and your greed will diminish even more and will ultimately disappear, making the world into a utopia. This concept may sound like a dream situation, but you can go a long way to realising it if you follow what I have said. You will find that life is more enjoyable if you refrain from going to excesses. Giving to others gives more satisfaction than receiving or demanding from others.

Finally, believing in me and following my teachings is not only about praying to me. When you pray you remember my words and teachings. This benefits you in your daily lives, if you follow them. If you live and act according to the rules I have laid down, you will always think about me, so prayers are not altogether compulsory in reaching me. They do, however, have a calming effect and give you peace and tranquility. Remember also that my temple is within you. It is not necessary to worship at the temples on earth if you listen to the temple that is within all of you. It is good if you do go to the temple of your denomination because you can meet and relate to other people who attend, but do not feel that you are in any way distant from me if you do not go to a temple, as long as I am in your hearts and thoughts."

After this, God turned towards me and said, "Ravi, I believe that you have some questions you want to ask me."

"Yes, Sir," I said. "There are a number of questions that people have requested that I ask You. You have answered several of them already during your talk, but there are a few more that I would like to ask on behalf of all the people."

I looked down at the sheet of paper on which I had the questions written.

"In your world, why are there so many inequalities? Why is it that some people are better off than others? Why is it that some people have far less problems than others? Why do you allow this to happen?"

"As I said before, you are in control of your own destiny. What you sow you will reap. In many cases people have worked hard for what they have achieved. In other cases, you, the people, have allowed the inequalities to exist by giving some people undue power and allowing them to take far more out of the system then they are entitled to. This results in the rest of you getting less than what you may deserve. The resources are not unlimited. This inequality is for you to tackle.

As for the non-financial problems that people have, one only thinks of one's own problems. Everyone has some problem or the other. It is wrong of you to judge that someone else's problem is less than yours. Each person's problems are as real as your own.

You generally tend to create problems for your own self and hence you have to solve them yourself. As I have allowed you to be master of your own future, you cannot expect me to interfere.

I tend not to get in the way of your freedom of living your own lives. Sometimes when I see that you are finding it impossible to get out of the web of problems you have woven around yourself, I do give a helping hand, not to solve your problems, but to give you some space to be able to solve them yourself. I cannot undo the past and I have no intention of interfering with your future. I can and sometimes do help in the present. If you take advantage of any help you get in the present you can make your future better. It is all up to you.

Sometimes in your life you will have noticed that your situation has been excruciating, and you were completely bewildered, not knowing what to do. Then without any explanation, something happened to allow you breathing space in order for you to try to solve the problem you were facing. This is the only help I can give you. It is for you to finally solve your own problems in one way or the other. You have not been created to be like robots that only obey commands. You have to use your wisdom in making good judgments otherwise, this will be a dull existence for you.

The problem people have, which spoils everything for them, is that they are not satisfied but want more than their fair share. A great deal of discipline, sacrifice and control is needed. If you do not have these, you will always have the problems that are associated with this greed element. This is a sure way for you to destroy yourself and mankind. The time is approaching for you to take steps, to stabilise the situation and save yourself and mankind.

You must remember one thing – do not do things that can harm other people. If you want to do things to harm yourself, it's your choice. In such a case, you are the only one who will suffer through your wrong deeds. But if your deeds make other people suffer, then this is a sin.

It is too easy for you to excuse wrongful deeds that you commit by saying that whatever you do is your destiny which you have no control of and therefore no way of changing it. That is one excuse I will not allow you to make, because I'm telling you quite clearly that I do not control your destiny.

After a pause, God looked at me as if to say, 'What's your next question?'

I looked down at my notes to study the questions I wanted to ask. In His answer to the previous set of questions, God had given answers to various others I had listed. I was trying to find a question to which an answer had not already been given.

I found a suitable question that I felt needed God's enlightenment. "Sir, people would like to know, why You allow wars and other acts of violence to happen? At such times situations get out of control and catastrophes occur. Can You not help to avert such situations?" God replied, "Again the question is whether I control everything, or you control your destiny. All the terrible situations that cause death of innocent people is by your own choice and deeds. You can do a great deal to avert most of such situations if you really want to. I find, however, that your greedy self-interest hampers you. In most cases, you have to try to put yourself in the shoes of the other party to find out why they are doing something which perhaps annoys you. Instead of trying to safeguard your own interest, if you try to get to the root of the matter and consider it on a humanitarian basis, then it is possible to smooth matters before they get out of control. Greed and desire to have total control of other people is the cause of most conflicts. In all situations there has to be give and take. The priority should always be to make sure that you are not denying the other party their dignity, livelihood and their basic human rights. You should not only consider your own interests but those of other people also. This dictum is for everybody. Be reasonable in all respects, and solutions that are in the interest of everybody will be found. Most people can be reasonable, given the chance. Be considerate about the needs of other people and their aspirations, not only yours. Solutions can be found. The situation is entirely in your own hands.

Why is it that people tend to fight for some small piece of land or some natural resources? All natural resources are there for the benefit of all mankind, not just for the strong few. These resources should be used to better the lives of all people. It is accepted that only a few nations and people have the knowledge, energy and acumen to deal with this, but why do these same nations and people want to keep all the benefits for themselves? Think about it. If the benefits are spread to cover all of mankind, all people would be happier and wars, quarrels and fighting would not be so common. No one has the right for total control of such resources. I have created them for the use and benefit of everyone.

You must also remember that due to your desire to live in opulence, the resources will disappear well before their due time, before you are able to find replacements for them. You are spending the natural resources out of all proportion to your needs. By utilising so much of natural resources and burning so much natural energy, you are also slowly but surely, destroying your environment. Curb this wastage before it's too late.

What I am saying is not news to you. You are all aware of the environmental dangers, the global warming dangers that you are facing due to the excesses you have allowed yourself. Even your leaders are aware and worried about all this and would want to do something to address the situation. Why, then, don't they act decisively to avert the dangers they know are around the corner? Again, it is a question of greed. There are vested interests that would not like drastic action to deal with these dangers. Profit and money are the root of all this. There are pressures on the governments not to act decisively. The pressures are so great that in spite of the need for quick and urgent action, nobody seems to do anything about averting the catastrophe.

A time will come when decisions will be taken out of your hands, and it will be too late to avert the tragedy.

In your world, money rules everything. Nobody takes time to think that money is not everything for a happy life. It is necessary, I grant you, but the importance given to it is ugly and destructive. It is time that you all woke up and realised that life has more meaning than the accumulation of wealth and money.

I do not frown on a luxurious and comfortable existence, but I do frown on the extreme vulgarity of the way some people live. It is a total waste of resources that could be used for the betterment of mankind.

I say all this to instill in you a sense of proportions. Your actions or the lack of them will ultimately harm and destroy you. Individually you may not be able to do much, but collectively, if you choose to do the right thing, you can change the world. Do not be afraid to try to change the world for the better. Unless you are willing, it will not change on its own. A relative handful of people hold the world at ransom. It is time such people realised that what they are doing is wrong. They have far more responsibility than just pampering their desires and filling their pockets.

If man works for the betterment of mankind, a society approaching the ideal Utopia can be achieved. It can only be done through collective effort. This can only be achieved when man has love for his fellow man as well as regard for his own ultimate happiness."

God looked at me to prompt me for the next question.

"Sir, people want to know why there are so many so-called terrorists. It seems that leaders of such terrorist groups may be mentally unbalanced, but how is it they can muster such a following of seemingly normal people? Cannot these same followers see through the people who incite them? What causes the followers to act in the manner they do, even to the extent of blowing themselves up to instill damage and death to innocent people?"

"I agree that all leaders of terrorist groups are mentally unbalanced, that causes them to do the horrible deeds that they do. But this is not only applicable to so called terrorist leaders. A great many of your own, so called, sane leaders also initiate horrible situations in the name of good. Tell me how can such actions, that take unnecessary lives, cause depravation and hardship to their fellow man, be justified, especially when they are carried out for material benefits?

Getting back to your question regarding terrorists; as mentioned, the leaders of such groups, without doubt, are unbalanced. They are not able to distinguish between right and wrong. They are hardliners who do not care about anything or anyone, but themselves. Unfortunately, they have managed to get a number of ordinary, simple people to follow them and do their bidding.

They are doing this and using my name as their excuse for their wrongful actions. They have distorted my word and teachings to suit their purposes to incite these ordinary people to carry out their terrible deeds in the name of the religion they follow. These people are being told by the terrorist leaders that by doing such terrible deeds, like suicide bombings, the people carrying out such orders will get a place in heaven by my side and that these actions are being taken in my name and for my sake.

Let me point out to all you people, this assertion is completely false. I do not condone such actions that take the lives of innocent men, women and children. The only action I condone is the fight against evil. Evil is not generally external, but within yourself. You have to fight against the evil that is within you.

There are people who carry out evil deeds, but these are misguided people who need to be changed into better human beings with love and affection. Some may be too far into evil ways to change them. If that is the case, then you have to fight and destroy them, before their evil ways destroy you. This action should only be taken when all other avenues for a peaceful solution have been unsuccessful. No one must be allowed to carry out such evil deeds.

The people who carry out such evil deeds have no place with me in heaven. They should not be under any illusion regarding this. This is applicable to the people who incite as well as the people who carry out the terrible deeds for them.

You may ask why I do not do anything about all this.

As I have said, the choice is yours. You can alter the world for the better, where no one would have cause to carry out such acts, if you do what is right and do not cave into greed at the expense of a decent and moral life. This is the choice I have given you. Do not let things slide to such an extent that to correct them will be impossible. Go out and embrace your fellow human beings. Look into their problems and make them your own. Do not allow greed to affect your personal judgement. Everyone has as much right as the next person to live a happy and adequate existence. Do not take this away from the more unfortunate people by making your own share far greater than others. It is not only a matter of sharing but of caring as well. It is a matter of taking out what you put in and no more. If you get more it is because other people, perhaps through weakness, allow you to get away with it. I say to all people, do not willingly give more than people deserve.

It is you, the people, who are to blame for such inequalities.

The people that are in a position to take out more than they put into the system should utilise their extra resources to better the world. They do this in the form of charity, but it is too little and basically uncaring, as it does not bring back the balance of nature to its correct position. Such people do not hand back even a fraction of the extra they have been given. If this continues, balance can never be restored, and people will carry on suffering needlessly. The general public can change this situation by refusing to pay high prices for their cost of entertainment, thereby reducing the amount being paid to such high earners. This will not be easy. People have to be willing to sacrifice their enjoyment and entertainment until such leverage is successful. Frankly I do not see this happening as the public will be reluctant to make such significant and prolonged sacrifices. A great many would rather pay than deprive themselves of their source of entertainment for any lengthy period of time."

God looked at me and I realised that He had finished what He wanted to say.

I said, "Sir, it seems to me that You are targeting the entertainment industry, as basically they are the ones who have phenomenal sources of income. Is there any guidance as to what is the limit that one should not feel embarrassed to earn, spend and retain?"

"It does not matter about the type of legitimate work a person does and how much is earned. I am against vulgar showmanship. It is one thing to live in relative luxury and another to flaunt your possessions and live in brazen extravagance. How many houses does a man need? How many cars? I think that you understand what I am saying. All this kind of living is utter waste. It deprives a great many people from living a very basic existence because the limited resources are diverted to where they are needed the least. The rule of nature is, 'for every action there is an equal and opposite reaction'. If your action is one of a destructive nature, then the reaction you will get will also be of a destructive nature. You must not channel your energies in destructive causes. Ultimately these will catch up with you to cause you more harm than you could ever imagine."

"Sir, what you have just said is going to stir a nest of hornets. There are some people who may take what you have said in the correct manner and do the right thing to readdress the situation that they are in. Others, however, are going to be livid. They will not give up their extravagant way of life. They are too used to it. They may make token gestures, but nothing else. I do not know whether the general public will make the concerted efforts to do what you have suggested. It would also require a period of sacrifice by them, before the situation has time to change. Will they have the patience and the strength of purpose to stick to their position until such time?"

"Ravi, is this a question, or are you just expressing your views?"
"I am just expressing what has come into my mind, Sir. It is not really a question, although if you can say something to explain then it would certainly be helpful,"

"I have already stated that it is up to all of you to do the things that will make the world a better place. I am not going to interfere.

I am just guiding you as to how you may be able to live a better and happier life. If you do not accept and take the chances you are given to change your situation, then you have no right to blame me for your troubles. You have to make the effort. Sometimes the effort will require a great deal of patience and sacrifice, at other times the results will be achieved much easier. Without effort, however, nothing can or will be achieved.

Talking about collective effort to achieve the desired results to benefit all; this also applies in the political arena, with regard to votes cast to elect your leaders.

I have seen, especially in the eastern half of the hemisphere, that the people tend to vote the wrong people into power, and then they lament the outcome. Why are they scared to vote for the people they want to represent them? Why do they, instead, let themselves be coerced to vote for someone else? Surely their strength in numbers is enough to repulse any force used on them.

People get what they deserve. They have the ability to have a better and happier life, if they use the tools at their disposal in the correct manner, without being frightened or intimidated. Unity is something that people have to learn about, in all walks of life, be it within the immediate family or the larger family of mankind. Think about it. The saying, 'united we stand, divided we fall' is very valid. The fingers of one's hand, by themselves have very little strength, but rolled into a fist is another matter. You have all been given the strength to deal with most of your problems. Take advantage of the remedies you have at your disposal."

"Sir, I think You have answered all the relevant questions that people would have wished to know about. There is one last question that I would like to ask. How should we live our lives and what should we do to live in happiness, peace and harmony with all our fellow beings?"

God looked at me and said, "I have answered this question over the course of this interview. I will, however, answer this as a separate and single issue to clear up any confusion or misunderstanding that all of you may have.

Firstly, you must understand that all of you are my children. None of you have more right to my attention or love than another. That means that none of you are any better than anyone else. Many of you, through your own efforts, have reached better levels of understanding and achievements. This is because of two main reasons; firstly, due to availability of resources within the society you live in, and secondly the efforts you put in that are necessary to achieve such goals.

You must understand that in many parts of the world such resources do not exist and therefore a great number of people cannot get to the same level. This does not mean that they are inferior. You are the lucky ones, they are not. It is up to you, the lucky ones, to create situations where such people can get the same level of advantage.

Your work is not done just because you have taken advantage of your circumstances to increase your knowledge and benefit yourselves. You have a duty to use your acquired ability and strength to try to give the same advantage to people who do not have it. You have to use your financial resources, your knowledge and any and all resources at your disposal to achieve this end.

Only in this way, over a period of time, can you eradicate the illiteracy in this world, which is the cause of misfortunes and misunderstandings. Unless everyone is educated to certain levels, there will always be problems for all. No one can be truly happy knowing that others are unhappy. You must realise that your own happiness lies in other people also being happy. It is your duty to see that others also achieve happiness, by making sure that they are not deprived of the essentials of life. This all relates to my talk on limited resources and people who take out of the system more then they are entitled to and give back very little.

You must not quarrel and fight with people of other religious faiths. All religions lead to me, provided the teachings are mine and not changed to reflect the wishes of various clerics throughout the ages, who have, seemingly, altered my teachings to suit their own interests. All of you are intelligent enough to understand what is rightly or wrongly stated by anyone preaching religion. Anything that causes friction and intolerance between various religions is absolutely wrong. It is not the religion but some people within that religion who make wrong utterances, cause friction. Do not accept this.

Live your life in a peaceful manner, allowing others the same right to do so. Do not force your opinions on others but at the same time, do not accept injustices.

Strive to better yourselves by working hard, but always be content with what you get. Discontent is a cause for unhappiness.

Do not compare your fortunes or misfortunes with people who you feel are better off than yourself. If you are going to compare your condition with anyone, do it with someone who is in a worse condition than yourself. You will find that, perhaps, you are not so badly off as you had imagined.

If you expect help from someone, you should also be willing to help others. You will find that the satisfaction you get by helping or giving far outweighs any satisfaction or pleasure in receiving. Try it. You will realise what I mean.

I will always be there by your side to comfort you and help you within the limitations I have set myself to interfere. I will give you strength to enable you to follow the right path, but ultimately it will be your decision as to the path you follow. Your destiny lies in your hands. I can only warn you regarding the dangers of constantly walking down the wrong path, as I have just done."

"Lord, can we human beings attain perfection?" I asked. "Generally, no," said God. "Only a handful will ever attain perfection, and they will be known as my representatives. Human beings can only strive for perfection, and this in itself will reach them to near-perfection. But being humans with human faults, they will not be able to sustain the total sacrifices needed to attain perfection. The act of striving for perfection is the nearest thing to perfection and in itself is all that I expect."

"Lord, I have a final question for you. Why did the catastrophes of tsunamis, Hurricane Katrina, the earthquake in Japan and other similar catastrophes where enormous lives were lost, have to occur? Why did you allow such events to occur?"

"Ravi, I have already given an answer covering such catastrophes. Not the specific ones you have mentioned, but catastrophes in general. As I have stated, I have no idea what will happen in the future, and therefore I am unable to avert such catastrophes, even if I wanted to. These catastrophes are generally man-made. If you interfere with the forces of nature and cause the balance of nature to alter like not dealing with global warming and the greenhouse effect, such catastrophes will occur more and more frequently. It is in your hands to avert the majority of such catastrophes by dealing with the problems as soon as they are apparent not wait until such problems have created the harmful effects. This is not to say that all catastrophes can be averted. Some occur to keep the balance of nature in check and to make people realise that more needs to be done to reduce the harmful effects of such events. Think about what I have just said, it will all make sense.

I want to say a few words regarding terrorists, including all known ones and others as yet unidentified. These people are evil. They are falsely using my name to attract innocent people from their religious sect to create terror and kill other innocent people, by stating that such recruits will be rewarded by me. This is false. They will never be rewarded by me and enter into my kingdom. These recruits should realise that the heads of such terrorist organisations are using them to carry out their evil deeds for their own evil ends. Their acts have nothing to do with justice, religion or any other humanitarian reasons. Such people are the representatives of the devil and should be treated as such by all sane and decent people, whichever religion that they follow. No effort should be spared in destroying such evil people. The world should make sure that situations are not created by actions and policies that create such evil organisations. Such organisations look for excuses to incite people to act in an evil manner against humanity. I want to tell all people that join such organisations, that they should not. In fact, they should fight against such organisations. Joining them and acting for them will not get such people into my kingdom," said God.

"Lord, I have now covered all the questions that I had. If there is anything else you would like to say, please do so, otherwise we will go off air and conclude the interview," I said.

"I have said what I wanted to say, which I am sure would have given mankind food for thought. It is in all your interest to think carefully and deeply about what I have said and act accordingly to avert the danger to your world and to make this world a better place for all to live in with dignity. Everyone has the right to a dignified existence. This will not be a one-time commitment but an ongoing one to be effective."

The interview was now over, and Roger came on air to close the broadcast.

After the program went off air, God went around speaking to everyone in the studio individually. Then He turned to me and said, "Ravi, I am going now but I will speak to you later about what needs to be done next. There is a lot more to be done to make sure that what I have said does not get forgotten and that people really do try to make an effort to improve the lot of their fellow beings as well as their own."

After God had departed, there was a great hubbub among the few WCN personnel present and the two families. Before Roger and I left the studio with our respective families, we decided to keep in touch to deal with the comments and feedback we expected from around the world.

CHAPTER 6

Aftermath

R oger and his family came round for dinner one week after the interview. When we all met once again, it was as though we had known each other a lifetime. There was warmth and friendship the likes of which I had never experienced before. I ushered Roger and his family into our lounge, where they made themselves comfortable on the settees. "What drinks can I get for you all?" I asked. Roger replied, "Whisky and soda with ice for me, thank you." I turned to Roger's wife and said, "What can I get for you, Elizabeth?" She replied, "Gin and tonic, thank you." I looked at Roger's children and asked, "What would you two like to drink?" David said, "I would like a beer, if possible, thank you." Jane said, "Orange juice, if you have got it, would be fine, thank you." I went to get the drinks for Roger and his family. I also got drinks for myself and my family, since I knew what they liked.

After handing the drinks to everybody, I sat down opposite Roger and asked, "Roger, what has been happening, during the last week after the interview with God? I am sure that there must have been endless feedback on God's direct talk with the people of the world." "You are right, Ravi, we have had tremendous feedback and thankful acknowledgement for our role in setting up the interview and creating a communication system never imagined or seen before. In this regard, governments, ordinary people and advertisers are asking if this kind of media coverage could happen again. Of course, that is impossible, as this required the miracles that were performed by God and will not happen again. The lessons learned in setting this up, regarding cooperation given by all the media and governments gives food for thought. We could never hope to achieve what we have just witnessed, but with such cooperation, we could achieve a great more than what we have been able to up to now. Perhaps that may be the future of mass communications."

I said, "I agree with you, Roger. I do believe that mass communication, as we know it, is going to change and go to another level. Perhaps this might result in closer ties and understanding, thereby giving the world the chance to correct its course of direction and saving the world from the catastrophe that God referred to. It seems to me that by arranging all this, God has, in His own way, helped us and shown us the path to avert dangers to the world."

"I never thought of it that way, but you are right, it is God's way to help us help ourselves. As He has stated, He will not interfere, but He will give us a helping hand if we take the opportunity to do so," said Roger.

"Roger," I said, "What feedback did you get with regard to the effect and impression of His talk on the people of this planet? Did the people really listen to what God had to say and are they willing to change their way of life to a better lifestyle in keeping with His laws? Did you get any comments from people who would have to make phenomenal sacrifices to conform to God's wishes? It would be very difficult for some people to do this as they have got used to their very opulent lifestyle. They will have to think very carefully about what they need to do. People who are totally materialistic minded will find it difficult to understand this. God has given everyone a choice, so these people will have to live with any consequences of their actions or non-actions."

"We did get some adverse comments from people who stated that it was presumptuous of God to interfere in their lifestyle. He had given them a choice and so it was up to them as to what they decided. But most of the rest were greatly affected by what God had said and felt that they would need to look into their present lifestyle and deal with it in a manner that would create a better world for people who are not so fortunate. They said that they would make a conscientious effort to tone down their frivolous and wasteful extravagance and help to make the world a better and happier place for people to live. A great many letters, telephone calls, emails and faxes have been received from people throughout the world who stated, almost as one, that God's talk had made them realise where they were going wrong and what they had to do to get back on the right track. How long this realisation will last is anybody's guess. At the moment they are embarrassed with what God had told them, so they are heeding His words, but once this feeling has gone, they will probably forget everything and go back to their old behaviours."

Roger paused for a few moments and then continued. "I feel that the only way people can be kept reminded is, as God has suggested, for you to go around the world and not let them forget. In time, if you keep on reminding them, it will become part of their normal way of life. I think we should discuss your travel throughout the world in this context and get started while memory of God's talk is fresh in the minds of the people."

By this time dinner was ready and we all went into the dining room. The food, vegetarian, was much appreciated by all. Once we had finished, we went back into the lounge and sat around talking in general before Roger said that they had to leave as it was getting late. On the way-out Roger said, "Ravi, I will start working on your travel agenda and arrangements in a few weeks' time, once I have cleared my desk of all pending work. As soon as I have caught up with my accumulated workload, I will contact you for a meeting to finalise the next chapter in this epic saga."

For the next few weeks, I kept myself busy at my workplace. I also relayed to my employers that I would not be available to work for them from a few weeks' time as I was going to travel extensively, perhaps for a number of years, to follow up on the interview with God. They said that they would be sad to see me go but understood the importance of the work that I had yet to carry out. They also asked me to keep in touch with them and to come and visit them from time to time.

While waiting for Roger to contact me, I spoke to God every night, getting His thoughts on the forthcoming world travel and how He wanted me to deal with it. What we had achieved in arranging for God's broadcast to the people of the world would be nothing in comparison to what had to be achieved in my world travel.

I spoke to God one night to seek His advice and help for the travel ahead.

"God, I need Your help for my mammoth task that is looming on the horizon. Apart from relaying the message You gave during the interview; are there any other issues You would like me to deal with during this tour? I also need Your help in conveying Your message to different people speaking different languages."

God said, "The basic message you have to convey is one of how the people have to conduct their lives, not always thinking about themselves but also thinking about other human beings who are less fortunate, and their needs to live a happy existence in a dignified manner. They need to realise that the world has been created by me for all of mankind and it is their duty to see that all benefit from my creation, not just the fortunate few."

God paused for a moment and then continued, "You have to convey to all people and religious denominations that togetherness is more important than creating differences that only lead to conflicts. Convey to all that I am the only God and the teachings of all religions and religious denominations lead only to me and none other, so why the need to quarrel and highlight frivolous differences in ways to reach me. Let them all pray and reach me in their chosen path, and not belittle anyone else's religious beliefs. Let people of all faiths reach me in their own way. No particular religion has more right to me than any other. Finally let everyone know that they are to be conveyers of my word and teachings from now on, so that my message is kept alive forever. This concept must be handed down through all generations so that no one ever forgets me or my word. Try to convince people who do not believe in me that I do exist and am there for them always. They will need to believe in me and seek me within their heart. It may not be easy as there are a lot of non-believers, but it is necessary for you to try. I cannot force such people to believe, the choice is theirs. But as long as they live the kind of life I have been outlining, it does not matter if they believe or not. In a sense such people do believe in me, without realising, because they live the kind of life as I would want them to."

God paused again to let everything sink in, and then continued once more. "Ravi, all of what I have said will seem enormous in its scope, but do not worry. I will be with you at all times. With regard to language problems, you need not worry as you will be able to communicate in any language necessary at the time. This ability will give you more authority and credibility in the message you are going to relay on my behalf."

Having listened to what He had to say, I was very much relieved and felt that I would produce the results that God wanted from my forthcoming efforts during my travels.

Finally, Roger called me and asked me to meet him the next day at ten in the morning.

When I reached WCN headquarters, I was told to go straight up to his office. Sally was waiting by the lift as the doors opened and she asked me to follow her to Roger's office.

Roger was sitting at his desk waiting for my arrival. When he saw me come through the door, he asked me to sit down in front of his desk.

"Ravi, thanks for coming. I have just completed the arrangements for the world travel of you and your wife. Seeing that you will be away from home for a long time, my family and I will be honoured to have your children stay with us. Our house is big enough to accommodate them without any trouble whatsoever. I have also made arrangements for both of you to travel back home from time to time during your trip, as I know you will miss your children if you stay away from them for too long. I hope that this meets with your approval."

"You have taken a load off my mind, and I thank you for your kind offer to look after my children," I said. "My wife will also have a sigh of relief when I tell her this. The children have been her main concern since she realised that we both will be away on this long trip. Now she need not worry as they will be in good hands."

"Good, I am glad that is settled," Roger said. "Now getting on to the details of your impending trip, it is going to cost the WCN far less than I had imagined."

"How is that possible?"

"The interview with God and now your travel to spread the message of God has caught everyone's imagination, not least the travel industry. One of the major airline companies is willing to fly you to all your destinations. And to places where it does not fly, it will arrange for its partner airlines to take you there. It is a complimentary offer by the company. Also, a major international chain of hotels has offered to provide accommodation in their hotels wherever you have to travel. Any places where they do not have their hotels, they will arrange accommodation in other hotels. All at their own cost as a complimentary offer, including food, drink and housekeeping services. You will travel in first class and stay in five-star hotels during your entire trip. WCN camera crew and overseas network personnel will be made available to you as and when needed. Now let us get to work on your travel itinerary as it is quite complex and will take a great deal of time to finalise since you will be travelling to almost every country in the world. Any comments on what I have just told you or should we start on the itinerary?"

"Roger," I said, "I appreciate the airline company and the hotel's gesture, but I cannot accept this extravagance after hearing God's speech. I request you to please apologise to the parties concerned on my behalf and tell them I have to decline such an offer. Economy class travel and the cheapest double room in the hotels will be adequate for our stay. I hope you understand."

"I understand and laud your decision. I did not expect anything less. I will convey your message and ask them to respect your wishes. I do not think that this will present any problems. Now let us go and have lunch at the same restaurant as we did last time. We will continue after lunch."

We went out to the French restaurant and had a light but sumptuous meal. We chatted about the kind of sports we were interested in.

After lunch we went back to Roger's office and sat down at his desk.

Roger referred to various papers and documents on his desk and said, "The itinerary cannot be rigid due the nature of your trip. However, any date change of your itinerary will be adjusted by the airlines and the hotels as and when necessary. Your itinerary consists of places you will travel to, but not the dates, as they can change during the trip. The only fixed date will be the day you start. You can come back at any time to visit your children. You will need to travel in two weeks' time, so start getting your things together to take with you."

He continued, "I have set out the route you will take on this trip. It covers almost all countries. If any are left out, you can notify your sponsors who will book the tickets and rooms. Your first place of travel will be the American continents. From there you will travel to the Caribbean countries, then to Europe, Africa, the Middle East, Asia, the Asia-Pacific area, Australia and New Zealand, and finally back here for Britain and Ireland. This is a very extensive and arduous trip, but as God is with you it will not trouble you as it would all others. You will have total network, TV and radio coverage in every country you travel, so you do not need to go to each and every place in every country. The network coverage has been possible due to success of the interview coverage by all the networks. They all want to be involved. Besides this, the WCN crew, in any particular country, will be at your disposal at all times. All governments have been approached with regard to your visas and they are all coordinating to give you, a unique, permanent visa to cover travel to any country in the world on any number of occasions. You can see how that one speech by God has affected world cooperation. I hope that this is a lasting impact and augers well for the future of our world. Let us hope that people do not fall back to their old habits. However, this trip is precisely for the purpose of educating the world, not to let things slide backwards. I had mentioned that the WCN will pay you a salary during this period, as you will be instrumental in WCN program coverage on TV and radio. If you leave me your bank details, I will arrange for the salary to be paid directly into your account. I will take care of any expenses that your children may incur and deduct such amounts from your net salary on a monthly basis, so you do not have to worry about your children's needs during your trip. I hope that everything has now been covered. If you can think of anything else then please tell me so that they can be dealt with immediately, before the start of your trip."

I thought for a moment and then said, "I cannot think of anything you have left out."

I thanked Roger for all the effort he had made to make this trip possible and went home. Roger told me that he would be in touch regularly. The next day I informed my employers that I would be leaving in two weeks' time for the trip.

A week before having to leave my employment the office held a party for me and my family, to give us a resounding send off.

A few days later Roger gave me all phone numbers and other details of our sponsors throughout the world so that we could contact them whenever necessary. Now all that was left was to take the flight to America.

I talked to God that night and informed Him about all the arrangements. He was happy about my insistence on economy travel and hotel accommodation. I asked Him for His blessing which He gave, saying once more that He would be with me all the time during my travels and would help me whenever I needed His help.

BOOK 2

Trip to follow up interview with God

CHAPTER 7

North America and the World

The flight to New York was at 10 in the morning on Sunday from Heathrow airport. We were required to get to the airport 2 hours before our f light, for check-in and security clearance. We arrived at the airport 2 ½ hours early, accompanied by Roger in his chauffeur driven car. We all went into the airport for the check-in and stood in the economy class queue for this purpose. As it turned out the check-in attendant seemed to know who we were and came straight to us and told us to wait on the side while she issued us our tickets and boarding passes. She came back to us within a short while and handed over our tickets and boarding passes, which the check-in staff of the airline had been in possession of from the very beginning. It seemed to me that this would be the format for all our air travel – tickets and boarding passes ready for us as soon as we reached the airport, not having to queue up for them.

After collecting our tickets and boarding passes, my wife, Roger and I went upstairs to the airport shopping area and sat down to have coffee and a chat before going into the departure lounge to board our flight. Roger and I talked for a while about the trip and then it was time to say goodbye.

Before we passed into the departure lounge, we had to go through the passport check desk, where our passports were examined. This did not take long, as it seemed everyone knew us, and we were to be given priority clearance. We had a special visa stamped on our passports, endorsed by the U.N., to cover permanent travel throughout the world. After the passport check we went through a security check of hand luggage and a body scan. The staff were apologetic but said that this was necessary for security reasons, just in case someone had placed something in our luggage without our knowledge.

We went into the departure lounge and sat down, waiting to board the plane.

At 9.30 we heard the announcement, telling us to go through gate 5 to the flight departure lounge to board our flight. At the same time, an airline stewardess approached us and asked us to follow her to the flight lounge. As soon as we arrived at the flight lounge, we were immediately asked to board the plane, before any other passenger, and taken to our seats by the window in the front row of the economy class cabin. We did not know it then, but we found that the third seat by the window had not been allocated to anyone else but had been kept for us so that we could be alone during the flight to preserve our privacy. I felt that we were being given too much preferential treatment, but later I came to realise that this was helping me to make notes about my visit to the country in question and what I was required to do in that country, without any disturbance from anyone.

My wife had taken the seat next to the window, as she liked to look out of the window at the sights below when the plane passed over land. Soon the plane filled up and the plane was getting ready to take off.

Noticing that the third seat was empty and the cabin absolutely full, I asked a passing airline stewardess, "Excuse me, is the seat next to me going to remain empty all the way to New York? I only ask because every other seat in the cabin is occupied, and this is the only seat left empty."

The stewardess smiled and said, "Sir, this seat is allocated to you for you to place documents and papers on the seat, which you might want to refer to, for your preparations ahead." Before moving on, she asked, "Would you and your wife like anything to drink?"

I looked at my wife, but she shook her head, so I said, "No, thank you, for now."

Now that the mystery of the empty seat had been cleared up, I stood up and took my briefcase out of the overhead luggage compartment and set it down on the seat. I took out some papers to look through them. The sheaf of papers had a list of various religions that were practised on the continent of North America. Since the population of the United States consisted of people from all over the world there were a number of religions practised in the country. There were also several small minorities spread all over. The main religion is based on Christianity broken down into various denominations. These are mainly – Catholics, Southern Baptist Convention (Protestants), United Methodist Church, The Church of Jesus Christ of Latter Day Saints (Mormon Church) and Church of God in Christ. I shuffled through my papers to read about each of these religious denominations to get a better understanding, before I arrived in New York. Basic knowledge could come in handy during my work schedule. After having read the notes, I had made, I put the papers away and placed my briefcase back in the overhead luggage compartment.

At about 12.30pm UK time we were served lunch. After lunch we decided to relax until we landed in New York, as I was certain that our program would become hectic once we landed in America. Any rest we could get was going to be welcome.

About half an hour before the plane was due to land, the captain spoke over the intercom system, "This is your captain speaking, we will be landing at J.F.K. airport in 35 minutes, so please fasten your seatbelts until the plane comes to a complete halt. We thank you for travelling with us and hope that you had a pleasant journey."

The stewardesses started going around checking that the seat belts were being fastened. When she came to our seats, she said, "Mr. Dass, as soon as the plane comes to a halt unfasten your seatbelts and come straight to the front of the plane to disembark. Someone will be there to meet you and take you through passport control, to collect your baggage and through customs and security."

As soon as the plane landed and came to a complete halt, we got up and went straight to the door of the plane as instructed. After a short while, the door opened and the stewardess said, "It was a pleasure having you and your wife travel with us. I hope that both of you have a pleasant stay in America. There is a gentleman waiting on the other side of this door to escort you out. Have a nice day."

As we stepped out of the door a young man approached and extending his hand said, "Hallo Mr. and Mrs. Dass, my name is Richard. I am here to help you through various check points and to collect your luggage. Outside the airport there is a limousine waiting to take you to your hotel."

Outside at the passenger pick-up area, we noticed the limousine waiting in front. As soon as the driver saw us, he quickly got out of the limousine and opened the back door for us to get in. He then took our baggage and placed them inside the boot of the limousine.

I turned towards Richard and thanked him for all his help in clearing airport formalities.

Before driving off, the driver said, "Good afternoon, Sir, good afternoon, Madam, welcome to New York. This limousine belongs to the hotel and is at your disposal throughout your stay here and I will be your driver."

After some time, we arrived at the entrance to our hotel, in the centre of Manhattan. The hotel looked magnificent. We went straight to the reception desk to check in.

I said to the receptionist, "We are Mr. and Mrs. Dass. I believe you have a room reservation for us."

"Good afternoon, Sir," said the receptionist. "We have been expecting you. Your room is on the third floor, number 321. The attendants will take you and your wife to your room along with your baggage. The manager will come to see you in one hour, giving you time to freshen up after your plane journey. If in the meantime you need anything, please ring through on the hotel phone in your room. Have a pleasant stay."

The receptionist turned to the attendants and said, "Take Mr. and Mrs. Dass to their room, please."

We went up in the hotel lift to the third floor and into our room, where our luggage was placed neatly on the side of the bed.

I took out some money from my wallet and handed it to the attendants, who thanked me and left. I looked around the room, which was large, luxurious and well furnished, with comfortable chairs, a coffee table and a large bed with a bedside table on each side. There was a lamp on each table. A telephone sat on one of the tables. On the coffee table there was some stationery with the hotel's letterhead for our use, and another telephone. On the bedside table there was a menu for snacks and beverages, and a list of various services the hotel provided with relevant phone numbers. There was also a booklet containing places of interest for the tourist, together with important places in New York. The room had a large window, with the curtains open, from where you could see the street outside. There was another door that I presumed would lead into the bathroom; on opening it I looked into a very comfortable and fairly large bathroom with a shower and a bath. I felt that a mistake must have been made, as the room looked far more luxurious and larger than the type I had requested. I decided to talk to the manager when he arrived.

My wife and I had a relaxing shower and a change of clothes. While waiting for the manager to arrive, my wife and I talked about our flight, the priority service at the airport, the limousine service and finally the accommodation provided to us. The arrangements were beyond our imagination.

There was a knock on the door. I opened it to find a man in his late forties standing outside, whom I presumed to be the manager of the hotel.

Extending his hand he said, "Good afternoon and welcome to the hotel, Mr. Dass; my name is Peter and I am the manager of this hotel. It is a pleasure to meet you, Sir. I hope that you find your accommodation adequate for your needs."

"That is what I wanted to talk to you about, amongst other things," I said. "I had requested the smallest and cheapest double room for our accommodation at the hotel. Are you sure that this room fits the description? It seems a bit large and appears rather more expensive than I would have expected."

"Mr. Dass, I can assure you that this is one of the cheapest and smallest double rooms we have at this hotel. There is only one other room that is very slightly smaller and nominally cheaper than this one, but that had been booked some time before we had knowledge of your arrival. Generally, all our rooms are large and most of them larger than this one," said the manager.

"I will accept that, if you say so," I said. "I would like to thank the hotel for placing a car and a driver at our disposal. This will certainly help us getting around in order for us to be able to accomplish our mission in and around New York."

Peter said, "It is our pleasure to be of help in any way. The hotel has received a number of calls from people who would like to speak with you and wish you well. There is a great deal of publicity regarding your trip to America. I will make sure that only important calls are put through to your room, others that are from the general public, we will diplomatically deal with ourselves. Please let me have names and phone numbers of people you would want to talk to when they phone. There were two calls, earlier, that I am sure you would like to take personally. One was from Sir Roger, Chairman of the WCN and the other from the President of the United States of America. When they called, I told them that you had just arrived and were freshening up. Sir Roger said that he will phone you at 3.30 this afternoon and the President will call you at 4.30 this afternoon. It is lunchtime and perhaps you and your good wife would like to go down to one of our restaurants for lunch. We serve cuisine from various parts of the world, and I am sure that you will find one to whet your appetite. Please feel free to have whatever you like, with our compliments. I would request you to sign for anything you have so that the right allocation can be made. If there is anything else I can be of assistance to you, please let me know."

"Actually, we can start on our mission at this hotel itself," I said. "Please inform all guests and hotel personnel that I would like to talk to them at 6 this evening at a suitable venue, with regard to my mission. I know that all hotel personnel cannot be present due to hotel security reasons, but I am sure that a speaker system can be arranged for anyone not present. I am sure that the publicity being given to my mission to spread the message of God will ensure maximum attendance for my talk. Please make the necessary arrangements and let me know where this can be held. Also please have a pen and a sheet of A5 paper handed out to everyone attending the speech and have ballot-type boxes placed at the venue as well as on the hotel reception desk. I will ask a question, and I want everyone to write their answer on the sheet of paper and place it inside the ballot boxes. After dinner tonight, if you can meet me, I would like to discuss and get your help for my program in New York in the days to follow. Now we can have our lunch and come back in time to talk to Sir Roger and the President."

Peter nodded and we all left together. My wife wanted to have Indian cuisine for lunch, so we went into the restaurant serving Indian food, while Peter went about his business.

When we entered the restaurant, we were led to a nice, cosy table, where the waiter handed us the menu and asked, "Can I get you something to drink while you consider what you would like to eat, Sir?"

I looked at my wife to enquire what she wanted. She said, "Freshly squeezed orange juice for me, thank you." I told the waiter that I would have the same and also requested that a jug of drinking water be placed on the table.

While the waiter went to get our drinks, we looked at the menu. I ordered chicken tikka kebab as I was quite partial to it, whereas my wife, being vegetarian, opted for paneer tikka kebab. For our main course, I decided to have vegetarian, so we ordered aloo sag (potato and spinach curry), bhindi bhaji (okra curry), dal makhani (mixed lentil curry) and 2 nans (Indian bread) to share. The meal was excellent, in keeping with the standard of the hotel. Neither my wife nor I wanted dessert, so we finished off with coffee instead. The waiter gave us the bill, for which I signed, however, I tipped him with my own money, as I was not prepared to sign for this too.

We left the restaurant and went up to our room to wait for the two phone calls we were expecting. As there was still a little time before the phone calls, I looked through the booklet on the coffee table about New York and its places of interest to get ideas about what I wanted to do in the days to follow. My wife decided to rest for a while.

Just after 3.30 the phone rang.

"Hallo." Roger said. "Is that you, Ravi?" "Yes, Roger, this is Ravi. How are you?"

"I just rang to enquire about your flight and the arrangements at the hotel," said Roger.

"Roger, I was not aware that such elaborate arrangements had been made," I said. "Starting with the seating arrangement on the plane, keeping the seat next to me empty, then the help to clear all airport formalities, the chauffer-driven car for our use and finally our accommodation at the hotel; it was just too much and far beyond our expectations. The room is larger than we need, and the service is unbelievable."

"All of these arrangements have been done just to make sure you can do your work without distraction and wasting time unnecessarily. The use of a chauffer-driven car is very handy, if you know anything about trying to flag down a cab in New York. What do you plan to do next with regard to your mission?"

"I have asked the manager to arrange for all hotel guests and staff to assemble so that I can speak to them at 6 this evening. Also, the President of the United States of America called, but I was not able to take the call. He is calling again at 4.30. I know that I am on God's mission and with His help, I expect things to be smooth, but this kind of high-level activity and recognition is not what I wanted. I do not want to be distracted from my mission. I suppose I cannot expect anything less in America with all its razzmatazz. However, I will need to talk to God about this. I also intend to go about for walks in various parts of New York for the next few days, to meet and speak to the general public regarding the effect on them of the speech given by God. I also hope to meet various members of the clergy to discuss similar matters with them and get their views. Please arrange for camera crew to record all this for network broadcast so that people of the United States and the rest of the world are kept constantly aware of God's message."

"As you are going to give a speech to the hotel guests and staff at 6, I will make sure that the WCN camera crew set up their equipment to film the event for broadcasting to the American people. I will also arrange for camera crew to accompany you throughout so that all your discussions and contact with people is recorded for broadcasting. Please let the camera crew manager know your program in advance. The same manager will be travelling with you on your journey within America and record all relevant events throughout your journey."

We talked a few minutes more on general matters and after I promised to phone him daily with updates, we hung up.

I picked up the booklet on New York and looked through it, until the phone rang just after 4.30. I picked it up and said, "Hallo, this is Ravi Dass speaking."

"Hallo, Mr. Dass, this is the personal assistant to the President of the United States of America. The President would like to speak with you. Please hold while I connect you to him."

Another voice came over the phone that I presumed to be of the president. "Hallo, Mr. Dass, I would like to welcome you and your good wife to our country on behalf of the people of the United States of America and offer you my good wishes for success with your mission. I saw your interview with God as, I understand, did the rest of the world. What God had to say had me thinking deeply about where we are at this moment in time and where we need to be. Since then, I have been having discussions with members of my government to formulate plans on how we can try to achieve the goals God has set for us. I am sure, with you continuously spreading the message of God throughout the world, we will see a number of changes for the better in the months and years to come. I will do my utmost to make sure that our government policy helps to promote the ideals that God has set for us. It is not going to be easy, but we will start in earnest and hope that some day we will achieve, in a small way, the Utopia God had spoken about. I am sure that similar thoughts are going through the minds of most of the other world leaders. If there is anything that I can do to assist you in your mission in the United States, please let me know. If your travel in the United States includes a trip to Washington, then I would consider it an honour if you and your wife were to have dinner with my wife and

I in the White House. My personal assistant will give you a direct number to reach me."

I said, "Thank you Mr. President. I cannot think of anything that would require your assistance, Sir, as everything seems to have been thought of and done for us already. I am not sure whether we would be coming to Washington this time around as my mission does not necessitate the trip. I hope that you will not be offended, but the only reason for coming to Washington would be to meet you. This could be regarded as a personal trip, not directly connected to my mission and may cause people to question my motives for my travels. There will always be some people who would like to find faults with what I am doing to distract people from listening to the word of God. I do not want to give them scope or reasons to do so. I hope that you will understand, Mr. President, and forgive me this time."

The President said, "I understand, another time, perhaps. I will transfer you back to my personal assistant for you to get my direct phone number anyway, just in case you find it necessary to come to Washington. You may need it in some other context. Goodbye and good luck."

With that, the President transferred the call to his personal assistant, who gave me the President's direct phone number. There was noise of static on the phone, before and after the call from the President. I presumed that a scrambler system had been set up for my talk with the President to make sure that our conversation remained private. After hanging up I called room service and ordered tea for my wife and myself. Shortly after, the phone rang once again. This time it was Peter, the manager of the hotel, informing me that everything had been arranged for my speech in the main conference room of the hotel. Peter gave me directions on how to get there. I told him that we would be there at 5.45pm. Our tea arrived at 5.15, so that we had to hurry to drink it in order to get to the conference room on time. During lunch and in our room, I had thought about what I wanted to say to the people, so I was prepared for my speech. In any case I had prepared myself for this and the direction I wanted my speeches to take during my travels, long before this first speech in America, so I was not unduly worried.

When we reached the main conference room, I noticed the ballot boxes outside the doors, and a hubbub inside the room, which subsided as we entered. The camera crew was setting up equipment to film my speech. My wife and I went up to the stage, where there were three chairs and a rostrum with microphones. Peter was already there, adjusting the microphones. When we reached the stage, he asked us to sit down on the chairs. People were still coming into the conference room until just before 6. I am sure that nobody wanted to be late, so the conference room was as full as it was ever likely to get this evening for my speech. Peter started to speak.

"Ladies and gentlemen, friends and colleagues, Mr. Dass, who I am sure all of you have heard of, is going to speak to you about God and the need to heed His words and teachings and to spread the same to all of mankind. Please come to the rostrum Mr. Dass."

I got up and walked over to the rostrum.

"Ladies and gentlemen, first of all I would like to ask you a question, to which I want you to write an honest answer on the sheet of paper which you were given on entering the room and place it in the ballot box outside the doors on your way out. To others listening to me, not in this room, a ballot box has been placed on the hotel reception desk. Please listen carefully to the question, and be totally honest in your answer, as no one else, but you, will ever know what you have written." I paused for a moment for my request to sink in and then continued, "I assume that everyone of you had heard God's speech a few weeks back. This question relates to the content of that speech. Certain parts of it may have relevance to you. I want you to think carefully about what God had said and what section of His speech has direct relevance to your present lifestyle. Have His comments and suggestions of changing lifestyles, to make the world better for all of mankind, had any impact on your thinking? Do you intend to do anything about this, to follow His suggestions, or are you uninterested in making sacrifices and changes to your lives? I would like to have your written answer placed in the ballot box." I paused and looked around the faces in front of me. There was surprise and bewilderment on some of the faces whilst others, who had probably given thought to the speech given by God, seemed at peace with the question. I hoped that by the end of my speech those who had not given much thought to God's speech, would have come to a conclusion regarding their answer.

"All who listened to the interview with God, please raise your hands," I said. Every single hand was raised. At least everyone present had listened to God and knew what I was talking about. "I request all of you, who want to heed and relate to what God had stated in his speech, to spread His message to all you come in contact within your daily life and pass it down to your children for them to do the same in their lives, on a continual basis. In this way the word of God and His message will always remain fresh in the minds of all people forever. Gradually the world will become a better place for all of mankind. God has created the world for the benefit of all people living in it, not for just a lucky few, so go out and spread His word so that everyone can benefit and live life with dignity. I hope that those amongst you who are skeptical will, with careful and deep thinking, come to be convinced, before it is too late. Everyone has a part to play to make this world a better place. Before I finish, are there any questions you wish to ask?" I waited for a couple of minutes and seeing no hand raised to ask any questions, I said, "Please place your answer sheet in the ballot box on your way out. Thank you and have a pleasant evening. God bless you all."

With this I went over to where my wife and Peter were seated and sat down next to Peter, to have a few words with him whilst the people in the room left.

"Peter," I said, "Will you please arrange the collection of the answers and bring them up to me when you see me after dinner? Thank you."

I went over to the manager of the WCN camera crew to talk to him and tell him my plans for the next few days.

"Hallo," I said, "I believe that Sir Roger has put you in the picture regarding my mission in America and the part you will need to play. By the way, please call me by my first name, Ravi. May I know your name?"

He replied, "Thank you, Ravi. My name is George Baldwin. Please call me George. Yes, Sir Roger has informed me about your requirements on this trip, I will need you to update me with your requirements as soon as you are aware of them, so that I have enough time to deal with them. I will be travelling with you throughout the United States along with the British WCN crew. In other places like Canada and the South American countries, I will also be travelling with you but will arrange local WCN news coverage crew and local communication networks. Have you made any plans for the next few days?"

"Yes, George," I said. "I plan to cover shopping malls, various ethnic areas of New York in a walkabout to talk to people, plus general walkabouts in places that I find beneficial for the mission in hand, which I can only decide on the spur of the moment. We will travel in a mini coach, so that all of us, including equipment, can be together. I will contact you once I have arranged for the mini coach and the time for departure. Leave me the name and address of your hotel, along with your hotel room number. I will arrange to pick all of you up and brought here for us to travel together. I will phone you once I have had a talk with the hotel manager regarding tomorrow's program. In the meantime, good evening and I will see you tomorrow."

By this time the room had become empty, and my wife and I went out to have our dinner. My wife felt like eating Chinese food, so we went into the restaurant in our hotel serving Chinese food.

The restaurant was decorated in a very quaint Chinese manner, with soft Chinese music playing in the background. We were ushered to a table for two on one side of the restaurant next to a window looking out into the beautiful and well-kept garden of the hotel.

We both ordered vegetable spring rolls for starters. My wife ordered vegetable chow- mien and I ordered chicken chow mien for the main course. We did not have any drinks but finished off with jasmine tea. After finishing our meal we went up to our room, from where I called Peter and asked him to come up to our room as soon as he was free. While waiting for Peter, I switched on the TV in the room to see whether my speech at the hotel had been aired on the news. As soon as I turned to the news channel, I saw myself giving the speech. I realised that from now I would be recognised by most people, who listened to any news at all. I suspected that during my walkabout, people would be more inclined to talk to me as most of them would know who I am and the reason I was talking to them. It would make it easier for me to approach people.

It was just after nine, there was a knock on the door. I opened the door and saw Peter standing there. I asked him to come in.

"Peter," I said, "We intend to go for a walkabout, to meet people in places like shopping malls, various ethnic areas and generally wherever we find it helpful to our mission. A number of these will be decided on the spur of the moment, whilst driving along. A WCN camera crew will be travelling with us, so please could you arrange a mini coach large enough to accommodate us all including equipment of the crew. We will need a driver who knows New York well, as well as a permit allowing us to park the vehicle freely wherever it is required. You will need to ask the New York administration for this request for parking. I do not think that you will have much difficulty as all government bodies have promised full cooperation. We want to start tomorrow so please let me know as soon as the arrangements have been completed. Now, have you got the answers placed in the ballot boxes?"

Peter placed a pile of sheets of paper on the coffee table with a larger sheet on top.

Peter said, "Here are all the answers obtained from the ballot boxes with the summary on the top sheet. I have looked through all the answers given and have analysed them. I will make all the arrangements you require and will inform you as soon as they are made. Hopefully this should be done by latter part of tomorrow morning, as all offices open from nine onwards and it is a working day. I feel uncomfortable with regard to your walkabout and the security risk involved. Perhaps bodyguards need to be allocated to protect you. What are your thoughts on the matter? Your driver will be the same as the one who picked you up at the airport. His name is John. He is very sturdy and strong so he could be quite handy if the need arises."

"Do not worry, Peter. I have the best bodyguard in the business. People will consider it odd that a person acting on behalf of God would need any bodyguards. The general public would also safeguard us if it was required. However, I do not think that such a situation will ever occur."

Peter agreed saying that he had not thought of it that way and of course I was right.

Once Peter left, I picked up the sheets containing the answers to my question and looked at the summary that Peter had placed on top. The results, from the answers given were very heartening. Two people said they would do what they wanted and were not swayed by the speech they had heard; they said that they were already giving to charity and did not wish to do any more. These two sheets were set aside, as were five other sheets, which were from people who stated that they had not given much thought to the matter but were willing to consider it. All the others stated that the speech by God was an awakening for them. They had not considered the matter in the same light as presented by God, and after listening to God's speech, were ashamed of themselves and would be making a concerted effort to heed God and not waste the extra resources they had in frivolous and unnecessary expenditure, but to utilise them for the benefit of mankind. They felt that this small sacrifice would not make them any poorer but would enrich their lives with the knowledge that they were making a small contribution for the benefit of those less fortunate than themselves. I sat for a while talking to my wife about these results and the day, as a whole, and how we had managed to accomplish so much in only a few hours, of the first day of our tour. We were both happy that the day had gone so well. At about 10 we decided to go to bed, as the day had been quite tiring, and we needed a great deal of energy for the days to follow.

I lay on the bed for a short while thinking about the speech I had given that evening, the question asked, and the answers received. I also gave some thought as to what we had to do in the days to come in New York, when we expected to leave New York and where we should go from here.

I then prayed and talked to God.

"God, first of all I want to tell you of the result of the answers to my question asked in my speech today; two people did not want to know or consider anything, five people are not sure as they have not given it much consideration but are now going to consider their situation and heed Your words to do whatever they can. All the rest were in total agreement and would do the maximum they can to help those less fortunate than themselves. So far, the response to your speech and its positive affect is beyond my imagination." After a little pause I continued, "I want to have an austere living during my travels, because, after what you said in your speech, I feel uncomfortable living in the style and luxury that I have been subjected to, from the start of my trip. I feel that people I speak to will comment on this and say that it does not relate to the type of life that you advocated in your speech."

God replied, "I am happy with the result to the question in your speech.

It is a good sign for the future of mankind. Let us hope that the positive element continues and becomes contagious. You do not need to feel bad about your travel and living conditions on this trip. At the outset you had stated you wanted the cheapest room in the hotels you will be staying in; it is not your fault that your sponsors have only five-star hotels in their group. You are being given this service freely to allow you to accomplish your mission. Remember, I had never advocated that people should not live in comfort, only that they should not flaunt themselves and their wealth, and resort to wasteful and vulgar lifestyle. It is the thought that counts. You wanted simplicity but your hosts want to be the perfect hosts, not because of ostentations, but because it is in the nature of their business. You are not living in luxury but in comfort. Do not worry about it. Changing the subject, I liked your reply to Peter about his suggestion for bodyguards for your protection. They will certainly not be necessary."

After a pause, God resumed with a slight indication of mischief in His voice, "Your first day in America was productive and went off quite well. Your first speech given in America was not bad, although still room for some improvement which, I am sure, will come as you progress in your mission. Well, done."

I felt relaxed and happy. I slept well that night to wake up the next morning feeling refreshed for the day ahead.

I awoke at seven in the morning, to find that my wife was just coming out of the bathroom.

On seeing me awake, she said, "Darling, go and have a shower. I will put some fresh clothes on the bed for you to wear today. Shall I choose your shirt, tie and suit or do you have any preference?"

"No, darling, your choice is always excellent. Whatever you choose will be fine. I will just go into the bathroom, complete my toiletries, have my shower and be out within half an hour."

While I was in the bathroom, my wife had said her prayers. I wore the clothes and bowing my head, said my prayers quietly, thanking God for his trust and confidence in me and prayed that I would always remain worthy of His confidence and trust.

After finishing my prayers, I phoned Peter to let him know that we were going downstairs to have our breakfast and would be back in our room afterwards, waiting for him to give us the information regarding arrangements for the day.

We went down to the restaurant to have our breakfast. We both had fresh apple juice to start with and then my wife had a Welsh rarebit, and I had poached egg on toast. We also shared a pot of tea. Back in our room I looked up the map of America and decided that after New York, we would visit Boston, Massachusetts, and then from there fly to Ottawa, capital of Canada, before flying back to the United States to continue our trip across the country. I studied the map of America and planned on where and how we would continue our trip after Ottawa.

Peter knocked on our hotel room door at eleven. I let him in and asked him to sit down on one of the chairs in the bedroom and tell me what our program would be for the day.

"Your program, for the day and for a further two days after, has been finalised. Within this time, you would have covered the places you wished to visit in New York. Now the arrangements for today and the next couple of days are as follows: the mini coach has been arranged and will be here at one this afternoon. The permit for your parking has been approved and is displayed on the windscreen of the coach. John, the driver, knows the kind of places you want to visit and where they are. I suggest that you have an early lunch and be ready when the coach gets here."

"That is perfect, Peter," I said. "In the meantime, will you please phone George, the manager of the WCN crew, and inform him the earliest time the coach can pick him and his crew up from their hotel and bring them here? Please also ask him to have their lunch before coming here. I will write down the name of their hotel and George's room number so that you can contact him. Let me know once you have confirmed timings. We will either be in the Indian restaurant or in our bedroom." I wrote down the hotel details on a piece of paper and handed it to Peter, after which he left.

At 12 noon we went down to the Indian restaurant. We had a quick lunch, after which we went straight to our room to wait for Peter's call. We did not have to wait long. At 12.45 he rang and informed us that George had been contacted and that the coach would pick him and his crew up from the hotel at 1pm. Peter expected the coach to be at our hotel, at the latest by 1.45pm. I decided that we would go down and wait for the coach.

We sat in the comfortable chairs in the reception area and browsed through some magazines, until John, the driver, came to us. He said, "The coach is outside, and we are all ready to leave, Sir.

I have got your route planned but if you want to stop anywhere enroute, please let me know and we will make an impromptu stop."

We got up and followed him to the coach. George was there with his crew and equipment, and we shook hands all round before settling down on our seats. Shortly after, the coach pulled out of the hotel area and onto the road.

John first drove us to a popular shopping area. My wife and I got out of the coach, followed by the TV crew members with their equipment ready to shoot footage of my talks with people walking around and doing their shopping. As we were walking, a few heads turned to look at us. Gradually more and more people started to stare at us and talk amongst themselves.

We went over to a small group of young people, sitting on a bench in the complex, talking amongst themselves and eating ice cream. When I approached them, they all looked at me enquiringly. One of them said, "You are Ravi, aren't you? I saw you on the news last night. Boy, you really put your audience on the spot and got them thinking."

The others nodded their heads and said, "Yes, we all watched you on the news and were impressed."

"Yes, I am Ravi. I am glad that you watched the news last night. At least you will know what I am doing here and what my mission hopes to accomplish. Did you all see the interview with God a few weeks back?"

The young man who had first spoken said, "Yes, we were all together when the interview was broadcast on the TV channels. We were amazed at the miracle that God performed to make it possible. I can tell you that the whole concept and magnitude of the occasion was awesome."

"How were you affected by what God said in his speech?" I asked. "Did it make sense to you? How did you feel at the time? How do you feel now, after having had some time to absorb and reflect on what was said?"

The young man, who seemed to be the leader of the group, once again answered, "After the broadcast was over, we discussed the speech given by God, and it made us think about where we are at this point in time, where we want to go and what we have to do to get there. What God said made a lot of sense. We are young and we have yet to live our lives, and if we don't heed the word of God, we are not going to have a world worth living in. I don't know what the older generation intends to do, but if we, the young people, don't do something, then the world is doomed and, with it, so are we. We have all decided to try to behave in the manner God wants us to. We are fed up with fighting amongst ourselves and the rest of the world, to retain our possessions and advantages and being afraid of losing them. The speech made us think that if the same advantages of education, health and opportunity for betterment were given to others who are deprived of these essential elements of life, we need not be afraid as there would be no need for anyone to snatch these away from us. More people will be content, making it a better world for us all to live in. This feeling, of thinking about others and not only about ourselves, impressed itself on our minds only after listening to God's speech. I don't know about other people, but for me and my friends that speech has changed our lives. It has made us think how we as individuals or as a group, can make this world a better place for all. It is a tall order and will be very difficult to accomplish, even if the majority of advantaged people thought in the same manner, but we have to make a start before it is too late.

My friends and I have decided that we will do all we can to help in this transformation of the world, be it in the way of donations in the right areas or by participating in activities related to achieving our desired goal. You had mentioned in your speech last night that you want people to go and convince others and spread the word of God. Well, that will be part of our activity. And I think that you will find that a number of young people throughout the world will feel the same. We are the future of this world, but if there is no world, what future can there be?"

"That is good to hear," I said. "I do not know how many people feel the same way, but if you and others like you, go around and spread the teachings of God, then more people will have a change of heart, thereby giving the world a better chance to stop the rot and save itself from destruction. God has asked me to tell the people to spread His message continuously, so that people do not forget His word. You have decided to do this without any request from me. This, in itself, is a good sign of the impact of God's speech. I hope that many people will be as proactive as you are."

"Well, we don't have any choice, do we? It is that or nothing," said the young man.

I realised that the young man in front of me had a great deal of maturity and wisdom for his age. It seemed that God's speech had opened people's mind to the reality of their situation.

After having spoken to this group, we walked about the complex talking to other people, individually or in groups. We found a mixed response. Some, like the first group of young people we spoke to, were of the same opinion, whereas others were not too concerned and wanted to be left alone to live their lives as they chose. These were the people who had to be convinced. The people I spoke to in this shopping complex and along the streets nearby, were generally from the middle- and upper-class section of society, most of them white. Now I wanted to meet people from other ethnic groups as well as people who were from the disadvantaged section of society. This would enable me to have a better picture of what people from different sections of society were thinking after listening to God's speech.

By this time, it was nearly 6.30 in the evening, so we decided to call it a day and go back to our hotels. The next day, we would be starting earlier, at 9.30 in the morning, so that we could get in a full day to talk to people and get their views. John dropped off the WCN TV crew at their hotel and then drove us back to ours. Before getting off, George told me to watch the 10pm news that night as our walkabout would be broadcast at that time.

At the hotel, before dinner, I phoned Peter and told him of our plans for the next two days. On the third day we intended to take the coach to Boston, Massachusetts, from where we would fly to Ottawa, before flying back to New York to continue our journey to other parts of America. I told him that I did not know how long we would be in Boston, as we would only be free to leave once, we had accomplished our mission in Boston. I would phone Peter from Ottawa when we were to leave for New York so that he could arrange for us to be picked up and brought back to the hotel. We would stay one night in New York to plan our coach trip from there to other parts of America. I also asked him to inform the hotel in Boston, so that our room could be made available. Finally, I asked Peter to have some sandwiches, fruits, soft drinks and flasks of coffee packed for the next day. We would eat our lunch on the coach or some bench in a park on the way.

Thinking about the complexities of our travel and accommodation at short notice, I began to appreciate the dedication of our sponsors to make our trip trouble-free and successful. Without their help our arrangements would have been in shambles. I would not have known what to do. These thoughts went through my mind very quickly and by then my wife had freshened up and we were ready to go down for dinner.

This time we decided to eat Italian food. Both of us enjoyed pizzas which we had not had for some time. At home we did not go out for meals too often, so our trip was giving us opportunities of tasting various kinds of dishes. The only criteria were that, for my wife the food had to be vegetarian, so it narrowed down the types of cuisines we could try, as not all had many vegetarian options.

We decided to have a little wine with our meal this time and as we both enjoyed sweet white wine, we ordered a bottle of Chablis. We ordered minestrone soup to start with followed by a pizza topped with lots of vegetables for my wife and one with chicken, pepperoni and vegetables for me. After our meal we had cappuccino.

Back in our room, I sat down on the settee and dialed George at his hotel. The hotel receptionist put me through to his room.

"Hallo, George," I said. "I want to let you know what my plans are for the next few days. Tomorrow and the day after, we will be covering the other places I want to visit in New York. On the third day we will leave for Boston by coach. I'm not yet sure how long we will stay in Boston; it all depends on how long it takes us to cover the area for our work. Once we have finished in Boston, my wife, you and I will take a flight to Ottawa. From there we will travel to various other major Canadian cities and finally return to New York. I will give you details enroute to Boston. You will need to contact your network in Ottawa for our TV coverage. After Boston your team can return back to New York to await our return from Canada. Once we come back to New York I will plan out our further travel from there. We will make plans for the rest of our American travel on a day-to-day basis, based on our need at that time. Tomorrow morning, I want to start at 9.30 in the morning. The coach will come to pick up you and your crew, so please be ready by 8.45. I have arranged for sandwiches and drinks for lunch tomorrow. Shall I arrange your hotel accommodation in Boston through Peter or will you do that yourself?"

George said, "I will talk to Peter myself with regard to our accommodation in Boston." Having said this he indicated that there was nothing else for him to add.

"Alright, then, I will hang up and watch the news on TV. Bye for now."

Once the news came on, the first piece of news was my walkabout and discussions with the various people we met. It was not a complete coverage, as the walkabout had taken a few hours, but it covered all the main points regarding our mission that I wanted people to hear, to get the essence of God's message and their reactions to it. George had edited the footage perfectly so that all points were covered without being unduly long. Most of the reactions were positive, some needed further work. This would be carried out by the young people we had met and had indicated their desire to spread God's message. Once they had seen the TV coverage, they would know whom to approach in this regard.

Things seem to be going according to plan, and the responses were fairly satisfactory. I did not expect to have 100% positive results, so I was not disappointed with the outcome of my first contact with the ordinary people of New York. That would have been too optimistic. The results we had to date were reasonable, with further scope for improvement once people started, in earnest, to spread God's message.

I talked to God that night, before going to sleep, to apprise Him of the events of the day. It seemed that people were taking notice and were ready to play their part to make the world a better place to live in for all people, not just the privileged few.

God said, "It is good that you feel things seem to be satisfactory and are going in the right direction. You have spoken to only a few people, mainly the ones who responded in a positive manner. You have yet to meet and hear from people who are disgruntled and are angry with what I said. You will be meeting them shortly. As you get deeper into your journey you will encounter more and more of such people. Hard work will be necessary to convince such people. This trip is not going to be as easy or smooth as you may think. You will have to keep your wits about you and use the right words, very carefully, to convince such people. It is the nature of this world that some people will never be convinced, however hard you try. If you can convince the majority, then such people will have very little effect on the world. Do not worry at the moment, do whatever is necessary. Such people will always be there and there is not much anything can be done about it. As I have stated, the choice is yours, you live and die by your choice."

After having talked to God, I went to sleep, as we had a busy day tomorrow which required an early start. My wife was already asleep.

I woke up early the next morning at 6 and had first use of the bathroom. I came out, after having had my shower, and noticed that my wife was up and had put my clothes at the foot of the bed. I quickly got dressed and waited for my wife to come out of the bathroom and get dressed. By the time we were both ready, it was 7.30, almost time to go down for breakfast. We left our room for the restaurant, just before 8. We had a quick, substantial breakfast, to fortify us for the day and returned to our room to collect a few personal things. While in the room I phoned Peter to ask him whether our packed lunch was ready. He told me that it was and would be placed in the coach once it had arrived at the hotel. We then went downstairs to the reception area to wait for the coach.

When the coach arrived, four hotel staff put some food containers, thermos flasks, plastic plates, cups, glasses and ice boxes which presumably had the soft drinks, into our coach.

John then came to us and said we could get underway.

We went with John and got into the coach, greeting everyone already seated inside.

Once John got behind the wheel of the coach, he said, "Mr. Dass, I'm aware of the places you want to visit. Shall I take you to these places in the order that they are easiest and quickest to reach, or do you have your own route preference?"

I said, "Since you know New York and its places far better than I do, your suggestion as to the route we should take is very welcome, so I am happy to be guided by you, thank you."

John said, "The places we will be visiting in the next two days are, the Chinese community in China Town, the immigrant ethnic groups and the Black American community in Harlem and areas where the extreme poor and underprivileged Americans live in New York, the Bronx, in that order. Apart from these, if there is any other particular place you have in mind, or you want an ad-hoc stop anywhere on our route, please let me know."

I felt that the itinerary that John had just outlined was suitable, as it allowed me to talk to some ethnic groups. Many of the ethnic groups, like Asian Indians were fully integrated into the community and could be spoken to in walkabout in normal areas.

In China Town, we got out of the coach together with the WCN crew to walk around to speak to people in the crowded street.

I noticed four middle aged women standing on the pavement talking amongst themselves. I thought it might be worth starting my talks here. I went up to them and stood silently a short distance away. They were too engrossed with their conversation and did not notice me, until one of them caught sight of me from the corner of her eye and stopped talking. She indicated to the others that I was standing there, looking at them. They all turned to face me at the same time and, the one who seemed to be the oldest said in a hostile voice, "Why you stare?"

I said, "I am sorry, ladies, I did not mean to stare, I just wanted to have a word with you."

They kept looking at me and all of a sudden, they noticed the cameraman behind me filming the proceedings and their faces, registering recognition, softened.

"I recognise you, you Ravi, the man on TV news last night," said the lady who had first spoken. "What you want?"

"Ladies, did you see the TV broadcast when God was speaking and relaying His message to all people in the world?"

"Yes, we did," said the same lady. "We Buddhist don't believe in God, only in deep insight to meaning of life and way of living, but on seeing TV program we think again, maybe is God."

"I am not here to change your beliefs, because God believes that your way of life and the Buddhist's search for the true insight to meaning of life, is as relevant as following His teaching. He wants nothing more from mankind than to think deeply about his existence and live life accordingly, because by doing just that, you are acknowledging His existence. What I really want to ask you is whether the speech you heard has had any effect on your everyday life and would you consider the points He highlighted and make this world a better place for all mankind? Would you be willing to make the sacrifices? Would you also convey this message to others and also to ask them to pass the same message down to others they have contact with?" Before she could answer I continued, "The purpose of my trip, to all parts of the world, is to convey this same message to all that I come in contact with, either directly, or through television or other media coverage. I do not think that anybody, whatever religious affiliation they have, would have any objection in spreading such message to better the world they live in, for the sake of all mankind. If you are convinced, then only will you be able to convince others." The lady looked at me, a little bewildered with the content and length of my speech, but she seemed to have understood the gist of what I said. She looked at her fellow colleagues and discussed something with them in her language. She then turned to me and said, "We all watched TV and agree with what was said. We and family and friends have changed since listening speech. We will do as you say and pass message on to all friends and people, we know to keep message alive. You do good thing by talking to people to make them change to help world and people of world. Good luck."

I thanked her for the commitment she had made. After leaving these ladies I went around several places in China Town and talked to people of various age groups, following the same pattern as with the ladies I had spoken to at the beginning. There was mixed reaction to the message given by God. Most of the people I spoke to agreed with the need to follow God's advice but felt that they would not have the time to spread this effectively, only to a few friends, who probably felt the same way as they did anyway. Others said that they would spread the message to as many people as possible. There were some who said that they were satisfied with the life they were living and did not feel the need for any change. As they did not consider any change in their own lives, they felt that it would be wrong for them to ask others to change. They respected what was said, but felt it did not apply to them as they were already doing their bit and were not willing to make any more sacrifices. During my walk, I only met people from the lower middle class to the upper middle class, but not from the extreme ends of the class of people living there. I felt that there may not be too many extremely poor Chinese, but there would be quite a number of very rich Chinese as they were very industrious. I had yet to speak to either of these. I would be meeting the poorer members of society on my visit to the Bronx, but, unless the wealthy themselves came to talk to me, I would have to deliver the message to them via the media and await their reactions.

By the time we had finished our work in China Town, it was time for lunch, so we decided to drive to a nearby park and have our sandwiches.

After all of us had eaten our lunch, we drove to Harlem to talk to the Black American population that made up a major part of the population there, plus other ethnic groups.

We parked the coach as we did in China Town, near the busiest section of Harlem, where we felt we would encounter a number of various ethnic groups. We found, whilst walking around, that the young people there seemed to cluster around in groups, perhaps for the sake of safety or strength. We walked up to a group of about a dozen young people standing or leaning against a building at the corner of the street. Their faces registered hostility, when they saw us approaching them. On nearing them, they noticed the cameraman behind me and possibly recognised my face, because their hostility was replaced by curiosity. On coming closer, one of them called me by name and asked whether I was there to talk to them about the message given by God, as I had mentioned in my speech to the guests in the hotel. Their attitude was no different from other young people I had spoken to, only a little more aggressive because they felt everyone had let them down, not giving them the opportunity to better themselves. They had few job prospects, considered outcasts by most people and treated with suspicion by the police and law enforcement agencies. They were bitter at the world which they felt had given them little in life. But they were positive about the speech they had heard from God, as they felt that His suggestions to create a better world for all was the only solution to get them out of their predicament. These young people were willing to change their way of life to instill confidence in people around them, they were serious about living a more respectable life so that things could change for the better for all. Through their change in attitude and way of life, having more respect for their elders and the law, they wanted to set an example for others in their community, so that these positive changes could result in change in people's attitudes, instilling care and concern for others. Walking around Harlem I talked to a number of people of all age groups and of various ethnic groups. Their responses, in the vast majority of cases, were the same. They were willing to make the sacrifices that they could, as they felt that such sacrifices would help others in the same dismal conditions as themselves and ultimately be of help to them also.

Analysing the responses I got from my talks to people in Harlem, I realised that people from the more disadvantaged sections of society were more willing to make sacrifices to change the world as it seemed to them as their only hope to effect change in others to create a better world. It could shame the more privileged into responding positively to the speech by God, seeing the less fortunate making such sacrifices to help others.

Before we had reached Harlem, I had requested George to arrange the televising of a live speech I wanted to make that evening at the hotel, that could be broadcast all over the country and let me know at what time it would be aired, so that we could get back on time. I told him that as I was unable to speak to any of the rich people in New York, I wanted to talk to them over a live telecast to ask them the same questions I had been asking of people during my walkabout. I would ask the ones willing to give a response to phone or write to the WCN offices in New York.

Just before we finished our work in Harlem, George had informed me that the live telecast of my speech would be at 7 that evening and would be played once again after the nine o'clock news in its entirety. The local TV networks would be filming the speech.

As George and his crew were not required to come back to the hotel with us, John dropped them off at their hotel before taking my wife and I back to our hotel. I told George that the coach would pick him and the crew up at the same time tomorrow as today. My wife and I reached our hotel by 5.30, giving us ample time to freshen up and for me to prepare my speech for that evening.

By now a great many people may be wondering why my wife accompanied me everywhere I went, without participating in any major way. To all of them I would like to say that she has been my strength and inspiration during my meetings with people. Her mere presence gave me strength to talk to strangers I had never met before. I felt at ease when talking to people when she was by my side. Also having her by my side, softened people to my unsolicited approach to them, as they were better behaved, and more responsive, when they saw my wife standing next to me.

At the hotel, Peter had told me that local media television crew members were installing their equipment in a small private lounge downstairs. The TV news networks had been informing their viewers that I wanted to give a speech to the super rich of New York and if they wanted to listen to what I had to say to them, they should see the broadcast at 7 that evening. I was thankful for this because at least a number of the people my speech was intended for, would be watching the broadcast.

I had finished writing and memorising my speech and went down to the lounge to give my speech.

When I reached the lounge, the TV crew were at their post and asked me to sit down on a comfortable settee facing the cameras. They attached a small microphone to my shirt lapel. Someone came over and put a little make-up on my face, so that my face looked natural for the cameras. A coffee table was put in front of me to place my speech notes on.

The cameraman informed me that the broadcast would start precisely at 7 and a green light would come on, in front of me, to indicate that I could start giving my speech. When I started, I should look directly into the camera in front of me. I looked at my watch and noticed that it was nearly 7, so I adjusted myself on the seat to be comfortable and waited.

As soon as the green light came on, I looked straight into the camera in front of me and said, "Ladies and gentlemen, you must be wondering what I want to say to you. As you are probably aware, I have been going around New York talking to a number of people from various ethnic groups and various sections in society. To date I have only been able to talk to people from the lower strata of society to the upper middle class. I have talked to them about the speech that

God had given, and their understanding of that speech. I have asked a number of questions of them to which they have given me their answers. I am going to ask you the same questions to which I hope you will give me truthful answers. I have had a positive response to my questions, from the people I have talked to up until now, but their answers could be vastly different from yours."

I paused for a moment to let my words sink in and then continued, "I am assuming that all of you had listened to the speech given by God. In relation to that speech, I want to ask you firstly, what impact the speech had on you and secondly what steps, if any, you intend to take to spread the message. God had singled out the super rich in his speech as the privileged people who could, if they wanted, make a vast difference in making the world a better place. God does not admonish you for your wealth, because a great many of you have worked hard for it, but He does disapprove of those who flaunt their wealth and spend it in a frivolous, vulgar manner. This is not the right thing to do in a world where many people are struggling for a mere existence. God feels that the extremely privileged have a duty towards people who are in need. If the super rich made an effort, they could be instrumental in creating a better world where people could get educated, have employment, food on their table, and live in dignity through their own efforts.

I am aware that many of you already do a great deal, but is it enough, taking into account the wealth you have? You have to search your conscience to answer this. Do you need all that wealth for yourself? Could you ever use this wealth in your lifetime or those of your children, except in wasteful, vulgar expenditure? Are you willing to make the sacrifices that God spoke of in His speech, and to what extent? If you agree with what God said, are you willing to go out and spread His message to all those you come in contact with? These are my questions. I would be grateful to have your answers to these questions. You can phone or write to WCN offices in New York. I thank you for listening to me and hope and pray that all of you will do your bit to alleviate the problems that a vast number of people are facing in the world. Sacrifices by all and the determination to make this a better world for everyone would, in time, result in a world where there would be no extremes, due to which so many problems arise."

I indicated to the cameraman that I had finished. Before leaving the lounge, I chatted with the TV crew for a few minutes and then made my way up to my room. I saw my wife sitting on the settee, watching my speech on the news channel. When she saw me enter, she switched off the television and got up. She said, "That was a good speech. I hope you get the responses that you would like."

We went down to one of the restaurants to have our dinner, after which we took a stroll around the hotel garden before going up into our room.

I phoned Peter to let him know our travel plans after returning from Ottawa. I had decided that we would travel throughout the United States by coach only, as it would give more scope to meet people enroute. The trip would culminate in Los Angeles and then we would fly on to Mexico and the rest of South America. I told him that I would write down the detailed itinerary and let him have it by the next day. The trip in North America would last a number of months and hotel arrangements would have to be made in advance for all of us. As it was going to be a long journey, we also needed two full-time drivers. We would need at least three hours during the day for talks with people and the rest of the time in travelling. We would have snacks for our lunch while travelling in the coach and would be having our dinner and breakfast at the hotels. All our work would be carried out between hotels, during our drive. After every four such hotel stops, we would require an extra day at the fifth hotel for a little rest so that we did not get too tired. Peter was to give me the contact numbers of all the managers at the hotels we would be staying in so that we could contact them, if the need arose, to change our itinerary plans.

After talking to him, I switched on the television to watch my broadcast. Then I prayed and talked to God giving Him up-to-date news on the happenings of the day, including my broadcast to the super rich. I told Him that the people giving positive responses to the questions were mainly from the lower classes, who had nothing to lose but more to gain from people making the right sacrifices, whereas there was mixed response from people who were better off. This, I felt, was going to be the norm all through our trip. We would have to work much harder in conveying the underlying meaning in the speech given by God to convince these people. This was food for thought, making me think that I might have to change my tactics when talking to them about God's message.

I then went to sleep. The next day, before going down to breakfast, I phoned Peter and reminded him about the snacks for our lunch. He said that the snacks were being prepared and packed as we spoke.

The coach with the TV crew arrived on time and we left for the Bronx to meet people who were really down and destitute. When we got there, I was appalled at their state of existence and the poverty. It was hard to believe that people lived like this in one of the most powerful countries in the world. I saw the need for action to help alleviate this kind of poverty and help raise people's standards of life to a more dignified level. I talked to a number of people living there who felt that unless help was forthcoming from all people who were in a better position, their conditions would not improve.

We met and spoke to several people throughout the day and finally decided to turn back. After dropping the TV crew at their hotel, we reached our hotel, where we went straight up to our room. I had to work on our detailed itinerary to give to Peter. I requested a map of America, with the various states and main cities within the states, from the hotel. I worked on this for a few hours until I had written down a detailed itinerary. I then called Peter to our room and informed him that the itinerary was ready for him.

It was approximately 200 miles to Boston from New York, so if we left for Boston after breakfast the next morning, we would be able to stop enroute to talk to people and reach the hotel in Boston by early evening.

I phoned George and asked him to get to our hotel by ten in the morning to depart for Boston by coach. I also asked him if there had been any response to my television broadcast the previous evening. He told me that some response had been received but that the full response would be forthcoming by the time we returned from Ottawa; so, I left it at that.

We started off the next morning, arriving in Boston at our hotel that evening, after having stopped a few times to talk to people along our route. These were filmed by the TV crew for broadcast, as on previous occasions. We reached Boston and spent two days there to talk to people from various spectrums of Boston society to convey the message from God and to ask them the same questions we had been asking other people. There was also a live broadcast to spread God's message to the sections of society we could not meet personally. From there the TV crew members and the driver drove back to New York, while George, my wife and I left for Ottawa to spread God's message in Canada. The local WCN TV crew members accompanied us in Ottawa. Our procedure had become fairly routine to which we adhered unless there was a reason to change it. All responses from the live telecast were to be forwarded to George by email so that I would be constantly aware of the responses and make a note of them to arrive at a percentage conclusion of the results by the end of my North American journey. Such results would be collated for every country I was to visit to spread the message from God. We finally returned to New York from where we began our journey and started our travels across America to our final destination of Los Angeles. It was in California, that I wanted to meet the super rich from the entertainment industry, as God had singled them out in His speech. I wanted to know what they had thought about the message.

We travelled across North America, conveying God's message in the same manner as before, with the same request to people – to spread the message to all they came in contact with.

All this time I had been in contact with Roger, giving him an up-to-date account of what we had been doing and what we had achieved. Before we started on our trip across America, I had requested Roger to arrange for a charity dinner in Los Angeles, a few days after our arrival, inviting the wealthy people there, who I assumed would mostly be from the entertainment industry. He would be charging $10,000 per head, the proceeds of which would go to a charity helping the extreme poor in America. If these wealthy people were really willing to help make this world a better place for all, they would not hesitate to pay this charge. It was a drop in the ocean for them.

We arrived in Los Angeles on schedule. On reaching the hotel, we checked in and then went straight to our rooms to have a little rest, as we were all fairly tired. We had reached our hotel in the evening, so we arranged to meet for dinner at 8.30. I had planned to stay in Los Angeles until the charity dinner, after which, George, my wife and I would take a flight to Mexico and then to the countries of South America. The TV crew and the drivers would fly back to their jobs in New York. The coach would be left behind in California at the hotel.

The next morning, Roger phoned me to let me know that the charity dinner had been arranged for the following night in the main dining room at our hotel. The time was set for 8 in the evening, with my speech followed by dinner. He said that tickets had been sold out – 300 in all. I was amazed at this response. This would amount to almost three million dollars for the charity, after deducting the cost of the venue and catering. The money raised through that one dinner was staggering. Perhaps I should consider doing the same in every country I visited.

The day of the charity dinner arrived. I prepared my speech for the evening. It was short, simple and to the point.

I was in the dining room with my wife at 7.30. People came in wearing elegant and expensive clothes. They sat at the tables, according to the name cards placed in front of each seat. The table in front of the stage, table 8, was for George, his TV crew members, the two drivers, my wife and me. The dining room was almost full. The few empty seats were soon filled up by the time I got ready for my speech. The camera crew broadcasting my speech were strategically placed, not in any way obstructing the crowd gathered there. At 8pm, I started my speech.

"Ladies and gentlemen, let me start by thanking you for your generous contribution to the charity. I am sure that all of you must have heard the speech given by God with its underlying message to all, but you in particular. He had singled you out for a particular reason. I am not here to repeat His message to you; I am sure you are fully aware of it. I have a few questions for you that I would like you to answer, after giving it careful thought. You will not be asked to give your answers today, but to write to the office of WCN in your city with your answers. What was the meaning you extracted from the speech given by God and what message do you feel He wanted to get across to you? If you fully understand the reasons behind his speech, pertaining to you specifically, and the message He was conveying to you, what do you intend to do about it? What sacrifices will you be prepared to make if you were moved by His message and recognised the validity of His observation with regard to yourselves? Will you be prepared to spread His message? If you cannot fully remember God's speech, you can request the network for a DVD copy. I am not here to judge you for what you do and how you live; it is for your conscience to make your own judgement. I have been blunt and straight to the point, because I feel the situation calls for it and that you would want it that way, rather than my beating about the bush. I thank you for listening to me; enjoy your dinner."

Having finished my speech, my wife and I got off the stage and went to join our group seated on the table in front of the stage. When we had finished our dinner, a few of the guests came over to us and said they would consider everything that had been said and gave a well thought-out and responsible reply to my questions. When all the guests had departed, I thanked the TV crew members and the two drivers and wished them a pleasant journey back to New York, just in case I was unable to see them in the morning before leaving for Mexico and South America.

The next morning, George, my wife and I were driven to the airport.

We spread the message of God in Mexico and all the countries in South America, before moving on to the Caribbean Islands and further afield to spread the message of God, including a short trip back to the UK to see our children.

I have asked a great number of people, either through direct contact or through TV broadcasts, about their reactions to God's speech and whether they are willing to make the sacrifices God wants them to make.

Now it is your turn, the readers of this book, being from all over the world; what do you understand about God's speech and His message in that speech? Are you going to do what He suggests people need to do, and make sacrifices to help humanity and create a better world for all? Are you willing to help in spreading the message of God? I put these questions to you on behalf of God and in the interest of all mankind.

CHAPTER 8

Conclusion

Whatever I have written up to now, have been my thoughts as indicated by my conscience and my interpretation of those thoughts, based on my search for God.

What I have written is based on things that have happened to me and my family that has perhaps shaken my beliefs. I will try to analyse these feelings and thoughts to either strengthen my beliefs or give logical credence to what I am beginning to feel. I know that at the end of the day faith is the essence of all beliefs in God, so I want to analyse everything to maintain my faith, if at all possible.

Since writing this, a great many things have taken place in the lives of my family that have caused me to doubt the existence of God. Everything that can go wrong and cause anxiety and suffering has occurred and persists. There seems to be no end to this. Just when one issue seems to be resolving, some other problem with its own set of difficulties and anxiety comes along.

I have done a lot of reflection and soul-searching. My conscience helped me understand what God wants from us. This led me to thoughts of the conversation with God, and I have come to realise that belief in God's existence and the strength of prayers can make problems easier to handle.

At the end of the day, it is indeed faith that keeps us believing in God. Faith, that God will consider our situation and will give us some relief and help us to survive. Without such faith it would be very hard to have a meaningful life or to even want to live.

It seems to me that total faith in God and belief in His existence is necessary to maintain sanity and to be able to live in the face of all adversity and problems that human beings face. Some people have it worse than others, but most people do have the strength to face all problems just by believing that God is there to help them. Without this belief and faith, life would be meaningless. Even though I have immense problems, I am keeping afloat only because I have faith that God exists and that He will help me at some stage. Hence the title of this book, "Faithfully Yours".

Considerable time has elapsed since I put pen to paper and in that time a great many things have happened to give me a new perspective to my views and belief in God. The biggest tragedy I have suffered is the passing away of my dear wife, Shashi, after a prolonged illness. She was in hospital for 10 weeks and 4 days before she passed away in hospital. Most of that time she was in the I.C.U., responding very little to any external stimulus except in the last few days of her life. She must have been suffering in discomfort and pain, but she could never tell us. She was unable to speak as a result of the many tubes and tracts in her throat. Until about a week and a half after first going into hospital, before she went into I.C.U., there did not seem to be any reason that she would not return home fairly soon. But then her vital bodily functions started collapsing. It is at this point that I really started to have faith in God and started praying regularly for her health and well being. I have never been more religious minded in my life, praying for her recovery. It seems that, either God did not heed my prayers, or He decided that she had suffered enough – she had diabetes, her leg was amputated, was wheelchair bound and finally her vital bodily functions crashed. Perhaps God decided that she needed to be taken away from all this pain to a better world, with Him in His kingdom.

Up to this point in time, I was an agnostic, wanting to believe in God, because belief in God gave some comfort in times of stress. When I started writing this book, I tried to go deep within myself and tried to put down what my conscience made me feel and think, as to what God would want if He existed, but not really having total conviction of His existence.

Since Shashi's hospitalisation, I started to have full belief in God, praying daily, because I felt that was the only chance for her recovery. Perhaps my prayers were selfish, but I was desperate for her to get better and come home for our sakes, not really considering whether, in her condition, she would have a painful and difficult existence. I now feel that God had more concern for her comfort than I did. I was so devastated that I was not able to realise that her pain and suffering would have been prolonged unnecessarily. She is now in a better place in peace and comfort than she would have been able to experience at home after her hospitalisation.

During this period of prayers for Shashi's recovery, I have changed a great deal as a person. I have started believing in the existence of God, which I had not believed in before, with any firm conviction. Although God did not answer my prayers, the prayers have given me more strength, tranquility and calmness than I have ever experienced before. I no longer get angry like I used to do, from time to time. I am more tolerant now and am better able to face life with courage and strength. Our problems that I had mentioned earlier, no longer trouble or worry me, as I am now able to take them in my stride. All these changes for the better have resulted within me and I now believe in God, through the strength of prayer.

I have not prayed to a god belonging to any one religion, but to a god believed in by all religions. God is one for all. Sincerely believing in Him and praying to Him within one's own religious beliefs, will help one reach God as surely as people with other religious beliefs. God is one, regardless of whichever religion one is brought up in. Do not belittle anyone else's religious beliefs or try to force your religious beliefs on others. All religions have a right to God in their own understanding of Him, in the image portrayed by the religion they practice.

I am now certain, that God exists, and if your prayers and belief are genuine, then you will always be at peace with yourself and your surroundings, however many difficulties you may have to face. Remember, you are not the only one facing difficulties and problems. There will always be those who have more difficulties and problem than you, so you should always thank God for what you have and not ask for more, lamenting on what you do not have. With prayers and gratitude towards God, you will always be content and happy. Strength of prayer and belief in God works wonders. I have experienced this in my own life, since the passing away of my wife. If God did not exist, I would have found it impossible to cope with my immense grief, as I loved, and will always love her with all my heart. God has given me strength, courage and wisdom to handle this loss. When I feel anguish, I think of God and how He has helped my wife by freeing her from the pain and suffering she would have experienced on earth. The thought that she is in a better place, keeps me from breaking down because I want nothing more than for her to be happy, and free from pain and suffering. I only wish that God will hear my prayers and let her be my companion for all eternity.

AMEN – OM

www.ingramcontent.com/pod-product-compliance
Lightning Source LLC
Chambersburg PA
CBHW021642120626
46545CB00002B/665